A SIGN OF LOVE

Janet Enos Perez

To Mom and Dad for giving me so much love and to my husband Clifford, who gave me the support and encouragement to share my love.

Foreword

In writing this book, in talking to people who knew and worked with and loved and sometimes were annoyed by my parents, in thinking about them, picturing them as youngsters, seeing them as parents and now as grandparents, I've come to realize how really fortunate I am—and how really accomplished my parents became in coping with themselves, each other and their environment.

Neither my Mom nor Dad, growing up as they did 50 years ago, had any special opportunities or training, but they each had loving parents. Parents who, despite limitations and inconsistencies, wanted them, shared with them, and were proud of them. Had their parents, and their community, known more and understood more about deafness, their lives would have been richer and less frustrating. Mom literally was reared to be above criticism in everything she did, and Dad to be "normal" despite his disability. Their parents did not hide them away, nor did they react with embarrassment because their children were deaf. Mom and Dad were not raised to be cringing violets who thought themselves inferior. When all is said and done, they got a good start in life, and they made the most of it. It is with hope that their experiences, and mine as their daughter, will help those who face similar problems, uncertainties—and joys—that I've written this book.

CHAPTER I

Only First Communion, Christmas and Easter Sunday arrived with as much flurry as getting ready for the County Fair. Donna, my oldest sister, bossy but competent, at nine a miniature adult, took charge, telling the rest of us what to wear and making sure that Peggy and I found purses, clean socks and shoes. The boys—Gary five, Rick three and Steve one—raced around imitating cowboys or the Loop-the-Loop until Donna's threats that they'd be left at home were believed. First subtly, then with outward insistence, we girls pressured Mom to hurry so she would be ready when Dad pulled up in front of the house. With any luck, he'd leave work early even though it was summer and there was plenty to be done on Grandpa Enos' farm.

A cry "He's here!" sent all of us to the door to greet him. Dad swept through us, happy and laughing—our demonstrations of affection always pleased him, and he was almost as enthused about going to the fair as we were. But he gestured at his work clothes to let us know that he'd have to clean up and change. Despite his farm background, Dad was a spiffy dresser and insisted that he look his best whenever we went anywhere. While Donna made sure that the rest of us were properly attired and had everything that we needed, we teased each other with dares about the "scary" rides and who would get sick and who wouldn't.

The eight of us piled into the big, five-year-old red Buick—our "family car"—and with Dad at the wheel we headed for Orland, 15 miles across the hot, flat northern Sacramento Valley from the little town of Willows where we lived. I'm sure the temperature had been near 100 at mid-day but a breeze cooled our faces as sunset reddened the distant Coast Range. A noisy bunch as always, (the Enos kids were known to be extroverts), we kept our good spirits from erupting into anger or rowdiness—Dad, we knew, wouldn't like that, and Donna was there to act as a drill sergeant— the boys still boasting about prizes and rides and we girls giggling and teasing them for being little.

Reddish-gray dust sifted from beneath the Buick's wheels as we bumped across the field used as a parking lot. The fairgrounds was a swirl of color and there were people everywhere. Rides and prizes and shrieks of delight, noise and flashing neon, assailed the senses. Laughing, pushing, shouting people waving candied apples and beer cups and balloons filled the entrance to the Midway. As soon as we pushed through the turnstiles, Gary and I broke away, eager to get to the rides.

But through all the noise, human and mechanical, I heard Dad and Mom. "Ja! Ja! Ra! Ra!" They called. Gary pulled up short and so did I. Dad gestured towards Peggy, three years older than me, and indicated that she and I hold hands. Donna took Gary in tow; Mom and Dad took Rick and Steve. Thus arranged in pairs, we resumed our plunge towards the fair's excitements.

Eager fingers pointed towards cotton candy at the first concession stand. Donna, as the family money-changer and keeper of the purse, ordered feathery pink blobs of the sticky candy for each of us. Within seconds we were gooey to our ears, laughing and describing the tastes to each other and to our parents.

Suddenly I felt self-conscious and looked up. People had stopped to stare at us. Some of them were laughing, others pointing. Those in back pushed forward to get a better look. I glanced quickly from side to side; sure there must be some kind of mistake. Dad was bending forward, his fingers nimbly forming letters, symbols, words, and Mom replied and the boys laughed and made signs of their own to describe the sensations that they were experiencing.

The cotton candy caught in my throat. Past the concession stand I could see the billowing canvas of one of the tent shows. FREAKS in huge red letters caught my eye. I shivered and stared at my mother and father. Freaks? Is that how people think of them? I rushed to my Mom and grabbed her leg, hugging it as hard as I could. She wrapped her arms around my head and patted and caressed it.

The magic of the fair had vanished. Subdued and hurt, I stayed very close to my parents for the rest of the evening. I felt like a stranger in a foreign country or an earth-creature in outer space. As a child of six, not yet in school, I always had taken my parents' deafness for granted. Signing—the hand language of the deaf—was as natural to me as using my voice. That my parents were different—so different that they should be regarded with astonishment, or surprise—never had consciously occurred to me. I loved them but I was embarrassed for them—and being embarrassed for them hurt me deep inside.

Looking back on that incident, and on my childhood, I realize that my father and mother were exceptional—and very fortunate—people. Each was born deaf and went through life knowing that he or she would never be able to hear a single word. In spite of that they managed to do all those things that rural families are supposed to do: attend school, get married, work, raise a family, support a church, drive a truck, pay taxes, go to basketball games. But it hasn't been easy and the frustrations, particularly for my father, go deep and have shaped everything that he and my mother have done.

Deafness is a unique condition. Those afflicted with it from birth historically have been brushed aside and treated as idiots or misfits. Every time I hear the term "deaf-and-dumb" I get irate. Dumb, I know, derives from an old English root word and means mute, or incapable of speech, but over the years it has come to convey the connotation of stupid. "Deaf-and-dumb" to the person in the street signifies a mental as well as a physical handicap. On behalf of all those who are born deaf, I strenuously object to the terminology!

Because the deaf cannot hear, most of them do not learn to reproduce the sounds that become words and thoughts in the speaking world. Yet most deaf persons have healthy vocal chords which are quite capable of producing sounds. These unformed words, which many deaf speakers utter but never hear, put some people off. They often back away, assuming that those sounds indicate that the speaker is retarded or ignorant. The deaf person, in turn, cannot help but react to the expressions and manners of the people he or she comes into contact with. If he detects embarrassment, or displeasure, or taunting superiority, he may withdraw physically and psychologically. Those who counsel the deaf have found these situations to be quite typical.

The world that we live in shows too little tolerance for those who are "different." It creates minorities, not only by skin color and religion, but by handicap as well. Educators, medical professionals and the deaf themselves often refer to the "Deaf World" as though it were a walled compound or barrio that separate those who were born with the handicap from those who were born without it. Subtly, in fact, such a "world" exists, but its walls are invisible. Many deaf persons choose to live within it, held together by the common bond of their disability and the ways that they deal with that disability. Others reject that world as too limited, and forge into the "Speaking World," sometimes with disastrous consequences.

My parents and grandparents plunged forward to motivate and develop their lives, as normal as possible, despite the frustrations and anxious moments, into experiences that will never be forgotten and must be shared.

CHAPTER II

California's great Sacramento Valley was unirrigated grassland, green in the spring but brown and dry by late summer, and the mines in the foothills of the Sierra Nevada mountains still were producing gold when my great-grandfather Carriere left Quebec to join an adventurous older brother in the little town of Willows. Then as now, it perched above the flood plain, a center of commerce and the county seat, filled with large shade trees and sturdy old two- and three- story houses with dormer windows and red shingle roofs.

A land of opportunity, where land was inexpensive, if not in fact free, and the growing season long, northern California attracted immigrants from all over the world during the last three decades of the 19th century. Some, unable to coax a living from the soil or unable to survive drought years or the floods which periodically washed across the land, moved on. The Carriere brothers stayed. They were practical, hard-working, unobtrusive young men, outdoor types who, like their forbears, were firmly Catholic. They worked on a number of farms and ranches in the Willows area, including those owned by members of Glenn County's Spooner family.

Apparently the Spooners were impressed with the younger Carriere brother and gave him a number of responsible jobs. During the 1890's, it was not unusual for hired hands to live on their employer's ranches, and great-grandfather was no exception. While working for the Spooners, he befriended their perky, bright-eyed daughter Rose. This friendship between the hired hand, a vigorous young man in his mid-20s, and the little girl developed into a romance when she turned 16. Great-grandfather's marriage proposal was accepted and the two were married in the Willows Catholic Church.

Partly through his connection with the Spooners, great-grandfather Carriere was able to obtain some land close to the Sacramento River levee. My grandfather Wilfred Carriere ("Papa," as I've always known him) was born there and still lives nearby in a house he purchased 50 years ago. He was, by his own description and those of people who knew him, an active, ingenious and quietly ambitious young man with a knack for tools and a wry sense of humor that he inherited from his Gallic ancestors.

"He always wanted to build things," the Spooners remembered. His boyhood projects sometimes fell wanting for a lack of such essential ingredients as nails. Among his earliest memories was one of trying to straighten those bent beyond repair. On one occasion, when he was only four or five, he followed his father and several of the Spooner boys to the site of a building they were erecting. Rusty bucket in hand, he collected the nails that fell while the crew was working. Everyone complimented him on his industriousness, which "made me feel real good," he remembered. But when the work day ended, the men patted him on the head and took back the nails he'd collected.

"They thought I was picking up those nails just to help them out, but I wanted them for myself. I was real disappointed when I didn't get to keep them!"

So disappointed, my grandmother laughed, that when their own son Herb, my uncle, was a boy, and was busily building something in their back yard, and she commented to Papa, "I'm afraid he's using up all your nails. . . ." Papa immediately responded, "You let that boy use all the nails he wants! If we run out, I'll buy some more!"

Farming in the Sacramento Valley watershed in those days was at best a gamble. Acreages were kept small by the availability of water and the shortage of machinery to plow, plant and harvest. The Spooners and the Carrieres experimented with a variety of crops—wheat, milo, field corn, beans—and gradually cleared the dense, jungle-like growth that matted the land close to the river. Willows, nettles and water grass clogged the rich soil where the river periodically overflowed, creating a swampland inhabited by mosquitoes and frogs. Further west, on the flat sloping plains, "jackrabbit" land turned brown each summer. "But we knew it would grow crops if we could get water to it," Papa remembered.

From boyhood on, Papa worked on these ranches. By the time he was 12, the age at which farmboys qualified as full-time ranch hands, he was tanned and strong. But his parents, unlike many in the Glenn County area, insisted that he continue in school. The Spooners placed a high value on education; a number of the Spooner children and their in-laws were teachers in the small one-room schoolhouses distributed around the county. Papa walked back and forth to the one-room school in Glenn, a tiny crossroads community beside the levee southeast of Willows. As a teenager, he helped the younger children with reading and mathematics, as well as taught them such practical skills as machine repairs, whittling and hitting a crow with a well-thrown rock.

He graduated in time to enlist in the U.S. Army at the beginning of World War I. Although they could have used his help on the ranch (northern California farms are called "ranches" regardless of size) his parents supported his call to duty. His mother, however, shed some fearful tears and prayed that her son not be sent to fight in the trenches in France.

Whether in answer to her prayers or due to unpredictable vagaries of the Army's personnel placement system, Papa was assigned to a heavy artillery unit at the Presidio in San Francisco and remained there until the end of the war. He was discharged in time to get home for Christmas Eve. The Carrieres went to mass that evening and Papa, in uniform, went along.

"Heck," he explained, "I'd grown so much my old clothes wouldn't fit me. I had nothing else to wear."

A reasonable explanation, but it may not have been the only one. Being sparsely populated, Glenn County had relatively few young men to offer to the military and those who served were regarded as heroes. As a 16-year-old girl sitting in the choir of St. Monica's Church remembered, "In those days, when you saw a soldier in church, your heart went pa-tatta, pa-tatta, pa-tatta at the sight of him. Right away you wanted to know who he was.

"Well, I was in the choir upstairs, singing, when this particular 'soldier-boy' came in. Everybody leaned forward, trying to get a better look. He seemed tall and straight and very handsome. All the girls' hearts were palpitating, I can tell you!"

The girl was Martha Maisonnave and she soon found out who the soldier-boy was. From her perch in the choir loft behind the congregation, she watched for him every Sunday. However, she passed him without noticing him the first time that he saw her. As he described it many years later:

"My brother Isador and I were sitting in a Model T outside the church. We'd gotten there a little early and we were talking and watching people when this girl walked past. It must have been a warm day, even though it was winter-time. The sun was behind her and as she crossed the street, Isador exclaimed, 'Hey! Look at that French girl! You can see clear through her!' She must not have been wearing any underclothes, because, by golly!, you could!"

Gram later explained that slips weren't in vogue that year, and none of the young women wore them.

As 'the French girl' had done, Papa asked around and found out that Martha Maisonnave, who was to become my "Gram," had moved to Willows during the War. Gram was born in a small town near Monget, France; according to Papa, she got both her good looks and her stubbornness from her Gascon ancestors. Her parents had emigrated to the United States when she was a girl and set up a laundry in Sacramento just before the start of the War. A shortage of help "—all the men had gone to war, you see—" forced the Maisonnaves to close the business. They moved to Willows, where a number of other French families lived. As Papa once explained, "Different nationalities lived in clusters in those days. Artois was Germantown; the French settlement was Willows." A short while later, they obtained a small building and opened a laundry in Willows, using the ground-level rooms for washing and ironing, and the rooms upstairs as living quarters.

With Papa on the farm all week, and Gram in town working in the laundry before and after school, the young couple had few opportunities to meet and catch a glimpse of each other except on Sundays at church. But such deterrences could not continue forever. Like most small towns of the post-World War I era, Willows offered few entertainments for young people. There were bars and a pool hall for the more rowdily inclined, touring tent shows during the summer, and a community forum for the others. But most popular, in 1918, was the roller skating rink.

"My friends told me, you see," Papa remembered, "that it was one of the few places that you could go to meet nice girls. I'd been away and didn't know hardly anybody, so I was happy to try it out."

He hadn't skated for a long time and he admitted that he wasn't the best skater in the world anyway. In trying to keep up with his comrades, he lost his balance and skidded across the floor on the seat of his pants. Amid laughter, he blinked and shook his head, then tried to get to his feet. A pair of skates pivoted to a stop beside him, and a slender hand reached out to grasp his. "Would you like some help?" a girl's voice asked.

Still embarrassed by his fall, Papa shrugged, then nodded. It was the French girl. "Yes sir," he joked for years after that, "that right there was my downfall." The two skated side-by-side for a few minutes, then leaned against the rail to talk. By then, Papa had regained enough presence of mind to both introduce himself and ask the French girl, Martha Maisonnave, for a date.

The occasion was a Knights of Columbus dance, a "dress-up" affair featuring one of the area's best bands. Although heavily attended by young people Papa's age, it also drew married adults from throughout the valley. "I was only sixteen," Gram remembered, "and it was the fanciest thing I'd been invited to in my life."

Papa arrived in a new suit that complimented the weight he had put on around the shoulders and through the hips. Never a large man, Papa nevertheless was well proportioned and could handle physical tasks of many men half-again his size. He drove into town to get Gram and found her "—all dressed up and sitting in the delivery wagon in front of the laundry waiting for me."

In their little living quarters above the laundry, the Maisonnaves didn't have either a livingroom or a parlor. As Gram explained, "the only entrance was through the laundry and I was afraid your grandfather might not be able to find me. You see, it was a very special dance, and I didn't want to miss it."

A few months later, the Maisonnaves purchased a little house across the street from the cemetery in Willows and Gram, still in high school, got a job cashiering in a Willows restaurant. Papa, the second oldest of the Carriere children, pitched in to help with the spring planting. Like his father, he was hard-working and ambitious. But true to his generation, he became fascinated with machines. While in the Army, he had seen what heavy equipment could do and was eager to apply those lessons to the ranch. "When he wasn't working out in the fields," Gram remembered, "he was in the garage tinkering with some machine or other. He learned so much about them that the salesmen and the mechanics in town used to come to him for advice."

These interests and involvements, as deep-rooted as they were, didn't keep Papa from dating Gram. "I used to pick her up at the restaurant and we'd go out on dates from there." Gram got up early to go to the restaurant each morning and type the day's menu. Then at noon, she'd go in to cashier for the lunch rush, and go directly from school back to work to cashier until nine at night. "When did I have time to study?" she asked herself, looking back. "Well, I didn't. I just had to make time whenever I could."

Courtships in the early 1920's tended to be long and somewhat idyllic; Papa's and Gram's was no exception. They "—went together—" for over three years. As Gram explained, "Young people in those days couldn't just take off and go somewhere and earn a living. There weren't very many houses and it was hard to find a place to live. A man and woman, when they married, intended to stay together and to raise a family. Not many of them could do it on just a shoestring."

Consequently, Papa got to know his future in-laws pretty well, particularly Gram's mother Pascualina. "But," Papa remembered, "I couldn't talk to her father much, because he didn't speak English." Nevertheless, Papa was accepted into the Maisonnave household and Gram, on her part, easily won the approval of Papa's parents. As the "courtship" became a formal engagement and wedding plans were announced, the bonds between the young couple and their respective families grew even stronger.

Like many newlyweds of that day and age, Papa and Gram moved in with the groom's parents after they were married. "How did that work out?" I asked her, expecting a frown or raised eyebrow or sigh. But, "Oh! just fine!" Gram responded. "If there were problems, I don't remember them. Certainly nothing very serious."

Later, when I asked her to describe my own early childhood, or my sister Donna's, or Herb's, they too were "—fine, there weren't any real problems, you were good babies, you really were." Always the optimist, able to find a silver lining, she was both demanding and kind, a doer rather than a moper who could draw from deep reserves of hidden strength.

This optimism, manifested as it was in a belief in the future, enabled Gram to accommodate to many awkward and difficult situations. Housing was scarce and expensive to maintain in those early post-World War I years and it was not unusual among farm families for a son to bring his new wife home to live with him and his parents. There was work enough to go around and Gram was energetic and cooperative. Unlike many people, she could adapt to situations without compromising her own inner feelings.

This balance served her well during the early years of her marriage. The Carrieres' house was small, and Gram and Papa only had one small room of their own. It was, Gram told me, just large enough for their bed and a few pieces of furniture, since it also served as a hallway between the livingroom and Papa's parents' bedroom. I once chided her, "It's a wonder that you managed to get pregnant." With twinkling eyes, Gram responded, "One finds ways of doing things, you know."

Her pregnancy was, in fact, celebrated. Both she and Papa were eager to have children and the young mother-to-be was the center of attention. She and Papa moved to a small rental house a short distance up the levee from the Carrieres' home. My mother, Mildred Carriere, was born there on September 8, 1923, weighing 6 pounds 2 ounces.

Mom was by all accounts a "beautiful baby." Papa and Gram were justly proud—and worried, for the child contracted bronchitis when she was just a few months old. Much to the the relief of her parents and grandparents, and with a doctor's help, Mom pulled through. By the time she was nine months old she was rosy-cheeked and healthy. She was, Papa remembered. "both a wonder and a puzzle, so soft to touch."

Healthy of appetite but occasionally fretful, the new arrival spent her first year of life as most children do, progressing from crawling to her first tentative walking steps, learning to hold a cup and drink, crying over wet diapers, developing teeth and learning to chew. She was slow to respond to voice coaxings, however, and as she grew older Papa began to worry about this disability of hers.

He watched her and devised little tests so that he could determine how well—or how poorly—she could hear. He clapped his hands when she was asleep. Or noticing that she was playing alone in the livingroom, he'd rap on the window or enter the house noisily or call to her when her back was turned. By the time that she was two years old, Papa was certain that she was deaf and the knowledge saddened him. But he did not tell Gram. He must have known that she would find out sooner or later; perhaps he didn't want to shatter Gram's illusions about her "perfect" little china doll. That Gram didn't realize it sooner has always puzzled me. I'm sure that there is some truth in the old adage, "People only see what they are looking for." That her baby might be deaf never occurred to Gram and, as she explained, "Your Mom, of course, was an only child until Herb was born 15 years later and Dick was born four years after that. I was with her all the time. I knew what she needed and took care of her—she was hardly ever out of my sight."

Children learn from their parents, but they also teach their parents a great deal. Parenting isn't something one acquires in school. From the time that Mom was very small, Gram reacted by shaking her head, clapping approval, wagging No! No! with her finger, gesturing with open arms, hugging her and kissing her. Thus, by the time that Mom should have learned to speak, a system of communication already existed and Gram continued to use these gestures, never realizing that she herself was being conditioned to Mom's deafness.

But eventually even Gram had to notice that something was wrong. She confided in Papa and he admitted that he shared her fears. They took Mom to a doctor in Willows. After examining her, he confirmed that Mom was deaf and told them that she probably never would be able to hear.

"But he wasn't sure—he said he couldn't be sure," Gram remembered. Very little was known about deafness or its causes 50 years ago, and virtually nothing about the training or psychology of pre-school aged deaf children. Doctors were few and far between, and most of those who had offices in rural American towns were family practitioners who spent much of their time delivering babies and setting broken bones. Almost any rural family could come up with a "Grandma" remedy for curing everything from sterility to the gout.

Since their doctor had said he could do nothing for Mom, Papa and Gram turned to popular cures. Papa, I suspect, remained skeptical, but went along with them just in case they might work. Consequently, he supported Gram as she listened to and attempted to follow any and all suggestions that might restore Mom's hearing.

One such "cure" was an airplane ride. The flying machines of the 1920's were sputtering open cockpit biplanes that vibrated as they flew. Going aloft in one, popular myth had it, would cause the ears to pop and clear the channels that caused the deafness, especially if the pilot went into a power dive.

Papa found a pilot who would take him and his daughter for a ride. I'm sure that he hoped that such a flight would cure Mom's deafness, but I doubt that he really believed in it. However, knowing his fascination for machines and how they worked, I'm willing to bet that he enjoyed the flight, even if it scared her half to death.

A much more elaborate cure was offered by a San Francisco "doctor" who was experimenting with electricity. He advertised a series of treatments that would cure everything from insanity to gout. One of the Spooners was making trips to the Bay Area to see him and suggested to Gram that Mom might benefit from these treatments. Gram made a trip with this relative and the doctor, after examining Mom, assured Gram that his new "scientific" methods would restore her lost hearing if anything could.

However, the treatments had to be administered in his offices, he told

Gram. She would have to bring Mom in every day. Papa and Gram agreed that such treatments were worth a try and Gram rented an apartment in the City while Papa remained on the farm.

Every day Gram wheeled her two-year-old through city streets to the doctor. She never had lived in a city before and she didn't like the noise and confusion. Nor did she like the men on the streets and the way they stared at her and the remarks they sometimes made. She greatly missed her husband and the farm.

Here again, asked about it many years later, Gram looked back on those months living alone in an apartment in San Francisco without alarm. Like many people who seem able to cope with anything and everything that comes along, Gram pulls the world in toward her until the details are clear and issues small enough that they can be effectively dealt with. She made this move in order to benefit her daughter, who was extremely precious to her. If she worried about her own well-being in the city, her purse being stolen or her apartment broken into, she gave no indication of it. And as far as I know, she didn't try to take advantage of any of the attractions that the city offered. She could, I know, be stubbornly single-minded. She was a wife and mother from Willows, which to her was the most important place on the earth; she was in the city to take care of her daughter and nothing else mattered. Neither beaches nor parks nor delicatessens nor movie houses held any attractions for her.

The apparatus the doctor used resembled those later developed to give shock treatments to mental patients. Of course, the current administered wasn't nearly as strong, and Gram assured me, "Oh, there was no feeling. It didn't hurt Mildred." But as she described it, "I'd hold Mildred on my lap and the doctor would put these things on her. The electricity would make her hair stand right up on end."

Yipes! I remember reacting, picturing my own babies in my lap. I don't think I could stand it!

But Gram did, daily for almost three months. The doctor pointed out that after only three weeks of visits, Mom had improved. His testing indicated that the stimulation was working, and that Mom was beginning to detect certain kinds of noises. Gram was elated. But as the weeks dragged on, she realized that the "progress" was, in fact, ephemeral. The doctor was a quack and was milking her and Papa of hard-earned and badly needed money. Disgusted and angry, Gram packed their luggage and she and my mother returned to the farm near Willows.

Other attempts to treat Mom included having a doctor remove her tonsils and adenoids and visits to a chiropractor for a series of treatments. But neither had any curative affect.

"We finally realized that we'd just have to accept the fact that your

Mom was deaf," Gram told me. "We decided we would do everything that we could to provide her with as normal a life as possible despite her handicap."

But "normal" doesn't totally describe the amount of care and attention that Mom received at home. Most children growing up in similar environments at that time thrived on a healthy amount of neglect. They were given chores to do and spanked if they didn't get home for supper. But they also roamed free a lot of the time, playing in the fields, romping with their pets, climbing trees, swimming, fishing. The breadth and scope of their activities increased as they grew older—and, in some cases, ornerier.

By contrast, Mom was a home body. Gram took special pains to make sure that her child always felt loved and wanted. She dressed her with care, and made sure that her hair was always combed, her shoes laced, her hands and face clean. Various relatives remarked on how well behaved Mom was when they came to visit. "Oh! she had to behave!" Gram admitted. "I didn't want anyone ever to say anything against Mildred." Another child might have rolled in axle grease or tied the dog's tail in a knot or thrown rocks at a passing Model A, but not Mom. Because she was deaf and might become an object for ridicule, Gram wanted her to excel in such things as behavior and appearance. Rather than normal, Mom was "special." Even Gram's and Papa's relatives aided the conspiracy to make her seem that way.

"I know that I spoiled Mildred," Gram has admitted more than once. Of course, looking back, it is impossible to tell how much Gram may have crimped mother's inquisitiveness and natural initiative by so closely monitoring everything that she did. From a very early age, Mom accepted her dependence upon Gram and others.

It was not, however, a dependence that outwardly frustrated her, or caused her to become anxious or rebellious. Nor did it make her less affectionate. A college friend of mine, to whom I'd described my mother, once asked me, "Were your grandparents, then, quite rich?" I suppose that Mom was as spoiled as some little rich children who never learn to fend for themselves in a rough and tumble way are.

But all this "special" treatment couldn't keep Gram's child from perceiving that she was different. In those days, farm families entertained themselves by visiting each other, especially on Sundays, and Gram and Papa hosted a constant stream of visitors "except, of course, when we were visiting someone else." Mom was thrust in among cousins and nephews, nieces and playmates, and they romped and enjoyed themselves together. These interchanges occurred so regularly that almost the entire network of relatives—which included almost everyone in that part of the county—learned enough "home sign" to communicate with Mother. "This is another example of the world accomodating to her, rather than forcing her to accomodate to it."

Often, within that silent world that separated her from those around her, Mom perceived and made connections among objects or events that were more complex than anything her fingers could relate. One day, while Gram was cleaning out a washing machine, she found a nickel. She gave it to Mom and Mom clapped her hands with delight. She pointed to her cheek, made the sign for candy. Gram laughed and indicated *Yes, the next time we go the store you can buy some.*

While Gram finished cleaning the machine, Mom took her nickel into the house. "I finished what I was doing—I didn't pay attention to where Mildred was. Then one of the neighbors called me up and said, "Martha, do you know that Mildred is walking up the road?" She was headed towards Glenn to the store to buy some candy!"

Impishly, I asked Gram what she did to Mom for taking off like that. "Well, I don't know, I scolded her. Mostly I was just glad that nothing bad had happened to her."

"In those days," she continued, "no one worried about sex, murders, or anything like that—not in Glenn. But you see, Mildred didn't go to that many places, and she could have taken a wrong turn or gotten lost. Then what would she do? She couldn't talk, she couldn't tell anyone where she lived, she couldn't even hear and know what someone was asking. And of course there was the river. It could be quite treacherous."

On another occasion, Mom tried to follow her Grandpa Carriere to the garden which he'd put in near the levee. Because of the height of the corn, she couldn't see him turn and come back to the house. When Gram realized that her child was gone, she frantically started looking for her. "Of course, I couldn't call her—it wouldn't have done any good." Papa was nearby and joined the search. In soft mud, a few yards from the river, they found her footprints. "I almost fainted. I thought sure she'd climbed the levee and fallen in the river."

A few minutes later, Papa found Mom sitting beside a row of nearly ripe tomatoes. *What are you doing out here?* he signed to her. She smiled and signed back *Looking for Grandpapa.*

Throughout her childhood Mom loved animals, particularly dogs, and spent many hours with them. "They seemed to understand her, and she them, better than any people did," Gram once said. One of her favorites was an incongruous mutt (Gram called it "just plain dog") that Gram's neighbor Marjean Balch accidentally ran over in her car in front of the Carriere's house.

Mom rushed to the poor animal's corpse, beside herself with anguish and—surprisingly—fury. "She seemed to think at first that Marjean had done it on purpose," Gram told me. "It took us the longest time to calm her down. Your mother never did cry very much—only when she was really, really hurt."

As well cared for as Mom was, as special as she was treated by Gram and all of the other relatives, she had been quite restricted in what she had been able to learn. Except for "home sign," she had no language with which to express her desires and thoughts. She must have been, at four-and-a-half years of age, a shy, uncertain little creature with only minimal understanding of the great world that surrounded her.

Gram could see this. So could Papa. They realized, separately and together, that they could do very little more than they already had done to educate Mom. After talking to some elementary school teachers in the area, then to Gram's sister Marie, they decided to send Mom to a Catholic School for the Deaf in Oakland.

Gram called it "the hardest decision I've ever had to make in my life." She and Papa looked for other alternatives, but there were none. "You see, I'd kept her so close. I'd done everything with her. The thought of her leaving made my head ache so bad that I wanted to cry."

Papa, always the rationalist, level-headed and pragmatic, peered towards the future. He asked Gram what she thought Mom's life would be like if she remained in Willows and never went to school. How would she act when she became a teenager? What, he asked Gram, would happen to her if we were killed or injured?

Gram's answers to his questions "—convinced us that it was the right thing to do." Wouldn't she be able to come home and spend the summers with us? Papa pursued his line of thinking. Already, in her mind's eye, Gram could picture how she would cram a whole year's living into the short summer months. Yes, she agreed, Mildred must go to school. The nuns, she reasoned to Papa, would take very good care of their daughter. At the school she would soon make friends among girls her own age. She would learn all those things that children are supposed to learn— reading, arithmetic, history—things that Gram couldn't teach her. The school would be good for her, wouldn't it? Wouldn't it, Wilfred?

Of course, Papa agreed. Gram was stating out-loud what he had been thinking for a long time. When she comes home, Gram promised, I'll give her and share with her everything that we couldn't share while she was gone. This will still be home to her, won't it? And I'll make sure it's a happy home, even though she's going to be here for only a few months each year.

Once the decision was made, both Gram and Papa stuck with it. They filled out the necessary enrollment applications and Gram took my mother aside and tried to explain what they were going to do.

Originally, Papa and Gram arranged that Mom should begin her schooling when she was five, but the school informed them shortly before the beginning of the fall semester that they were over-crowded and couldn't take her for another year. "It was a real reprieve!" Gram recalled. "Oh! I was so pleased! But the next year came around awfully fast and I had to face the fact that I was going to lose her all over again.

"I tried to make leaving home easier for your Mom by making her new clothes and telling her how pretty she looked when she was wearing them. We celebrated her birthday early so she could have a party and open presents at home. She liked that but she still didn't understand why she had to go away."

But, despite a few tears, Mom accepted the arrangements—as she accepted everything that was arranged for her. Looking back, I wonder if her life and the things that happened in it were as puzzling to her as they seem to me when I try to project myself into her silent world. Though high-spirited, even mischievous at times, Mom never was a rebel—not outwardly at least. While she was growing up, Gram virtually arranged her own existence around that of her non-hearing child.

Yet she did so thoughtfully and unoppressively. I doubt that Mom, as a child, ever felt overly restricted or fenced in. For those first six years of her life, everything was handled with a velvet touch. Unlike the butterfly, that must fight its way out of a cocoon in order to develop strength enough to fly, Mom emerged without a struggle, the binding strings parting as she pressed lightly against them. Her dependence upon Gram and Papa was so natural—and so complete—that she didn't perceive anything unusual about them. As far as she knew, her life was the way all life was. She didn't fight against it, or worry about the details.

After all, the details would take care of themselves. They always had. And, as far as she knew, they always would.

CHAPTER III

A chilling fog muted Oakland's soot-stained buildings as Gram and Papa pulled out of the city without their daughter for the first time in six years. For a moment, on a hill overlooking the shrouded tangle of clapboard and concrete, the crowded houses shoved together between gray fences and grayer clotheslines, Papa pulled to the side of the road, ostensibly to check directions but in reality to look back at the metropolis that absorbed living organisms like some giant amoeba—absorbed them and disgorged them, anonymous and gray, to live out their lives far from neatly ploughed furrows glistening with irrigation water, stars overhead and the friendly laughter of relatives gathering over a Sunday barbecue.

But the fog and the uneven contours of the hills, prevented him from distinguishing the high walls of the Catholic school at which he and Gram had left my mother. Straightening his shoulders a little, he sighed and eased the car into gear. It was a long trip home, over rough gravel roads; he and Gram couldn't sit indulging their regrets. He put his hand on Gram's shoulder and she clutched it gratefully—almost desperately— as he pulled back onto the highway.

Thus in one day, their whole world and its center of focus changed completely. Even so, the change wasn't as drastic for them as it was for Mom. From being "special," the center of attention, watched and attended and catered to, she suddenly had become "another poor deaf child" to be fit into a system. She would wear itchy black socks, eat oatmeal and sit erectly in class, her head upright and her hands folded on top of her desk until the teaching nun released her to a more relaxed posture. She would stand in line, sleep in a dormitory, eat in a cafeteria. There would be no puppies running up to lick her fingertips when she stepped outdoors, no pretty dresses or fancy Sunday desserts. And no kisses, caresses, hands clapped in approval. Gram wouldn't be there to run to when a knee was bruised or feelings were hurt.

Gram, of course, realized this and wept many tear over it. She worried a great deal, even after getting assurances from the school that her daughter was doing "as well as could be expected." Gram took this to mean that the special deaf girl from a farm far away from the smoke and fog and rudeness of the city gradually was adjusting despite the strange and sometimes hostile environment in which she found herself. She made the sign of the cross and said a little prayer for her suffering daughter.

Like most people who are so sure of their way of life that they can't conceive anyone could be happy in any other circumstances, Gram was making assumptions based on her own—and not Mom's— personality.

All that Gram suspected about the school was true— except for Mom's reaction to it. The nun's report "—as well as could be expected—" should have been translated, "Mildred's just like the others were at first but in time she will come around." Despite the cold stone buildings, the regimented life style and the ugly black stockings that she had to wear day in and day out, Mom was, for the first time in her life, among people who reacted as she did to the world around them. Within the confines of school, she suddenly had become "normal" rather than "special."

As disciplinarians and as teachers, the nuns were unchangeable and old-fashioned. Few of them possessed what now would be called "special education" skills. Mom's Aunt Marie, acting as Gram's proxy, made frequent trips across the Bay to check on Mom's progress and was startled and somewhat disappointed to discover that the nuns didn't sign well. She dug through San Francisco bookstores until she found a book on signing, which she bought and gave to Mom. With it, and the help of schoolmates, Mom began to expand the "home sign" she had learned in Willows and develop a more universal, and expressive, silent language.

If the nuns were dedicated to conformity, obedience and order, the deaf children that they were supervising were even more dedicated to fun, disruption and peer group diversions. For most of Mom's new companions, life in the deaf school was a game; the gals there tried to get by with as much as possible without getting caught. No sooner had Mom crawled beneath the blankets of her little cot and snuggled her head against her pillow that first night at school than a hand touched her shoulder. *Come over here! Come on!* To Mom's surprise, nearly every girl in the dormitory had slipped from beneath their bedcovers and they were gathering near a window.

Forty years later, her face lit up and she laughed, describing the scene. The older girls, having returned to the school after summer vacations at home, had new stories and new jokes to tell. In the moonlight, their hands and faces barely visible, they nudged and laughed and pantomimed, spelling out words and events. Suddenly the girl watching the stairs darted for her bed. A hand grabbed Mom's shoulder and pushed her towards her own rumpled covers just as a flashlight beam swung around the room. Fortunately for Mom, it focused on other beds before it reached hers.

Hands around her shoulders, her eyes wide, Mom began to tremble. Tears filled her eyes. All she could see was the flashlight beam that looked as big as a searchlight. She waved her finger in front of her face, signing *It wasn't me! it wasn't me!* The beam poked closer, then swung away and Mom sighed, vowing that she'd never sneak out of bed again. But as soon as the nun had left the room, the older girls regathered and Mom, despite her resolve, joined them. Especially funny were the stories where Mom's new companions imitated the nuns with their stiff collars and long black gowns striding through the dormitory waving flashlights and poking fingers at girls stifling their laughter while they pretended to sleep.

Some nights, instead of telling stories, the girls would play hide-and-seek. In the dark, the rows of narrow beds offered plenty of places of concealment. Whoever was "It" had to touch those she caught; consequently, the game sometimes got rather rambunctious. To try to circumvent getting caught, the girls would post a look-out by the door to watch for the nuns. As soon as she detected a movement or saw the muted beam of the dreaded flashlight, the look-out would scamper for cover and the rest of the girls would follow.

In would rush the nun, determined to catch and punish the culprits. The rules of the school limited the amount of noise she could make, and the overhead lights were to be turned on only in case of emergency, so the flashlight was her only tool. The deaf girls all became excellent actresses, Mom once told me. She showed me how they would react when the nuns caught them: a startled, just-awakened-from-sleep cry, yawns, confusion, blinking eyes and finally *Not me! it wasn't me! I was sound asleep!* protestations in sign.

The girls were at a disadvantage because they couldn't hear or relate to the amount of noise they were making. But neither school restrictions nor the nun's continuing attempts to make obedient little ladies out of them deterred these night-time escapades.

Relatives could visit the school (except during classtime) and sometimes the girls were allowed to leave the school for an afternoon or weekend. One of the best things about such excursions, as far as Mom was concerned, were the "goodies" that could be acquired. When her Aunt Marie came to visit, Mom would coax her for candy or cupcakes or soda pop—treats that she couldn't get at school.

The school's diet was plain (although basically nourishing) and the students weren't allowed to have seconds. Consequently, getting something extra to eat was a big accomplishment, whether it was obtained from visitors or sneaked out of the kitchen.

Occasionally, the cooks at the school would bake cakes and each girl would be given a small piece for dessert. The rest would be put away for the following evenings. Knowing that, Mom and her companions developed an ingenious scheme for spiriting some of the pastry into the dormitory.

The girl's laundry was done in the basement. Each child's clothing was marked (in most cases, their initials or names actually were sewed into the waistband or collar) and the girls would drop their dirty clothes down a chute to the basement. This same chute went past the kitchen, which was on the ground floor beneath the dormitory rooms. Late at night, after the school was silent and the nun's asleep, one of the older girls would sneak down to the kitchen. Her companions in the dormitory would tie a string around a paper sack and lower it down the chute. As quickly and quietly! as possible, the girl in the kitchen would fill the bag with cake and the girls above would haul the prize up the chute. If the girls were caught in the kitchen after she'd loaded the bag of goodies, or on the stairs leading back to her room, she could plead innocent and maintain that she'd only wanted a drink of water or had been walking in her sleep. Then, when she returned to the dormitory, she and the others would celebrate with a late-night feast.

According to Mom's Aunt Marie, the nuns primarily were caretakers—religious babysitters—rather than trained teachers. How true this is, I don't know (the school long since has been closed), but I believe that her criticism is justified. I find no evidence that the nuns thought of their charges as potentially independent citizens who someday would strike out into the world and earn a living. Women weren't supposed to be independent anyway, and many nuns, especially those from Old World backgrounds, saw marriage and the convent as the only alternatives open to a young woman. They seemed to reflect the attitude that deaf children would always be dependent and could best serve society by acquiring a few domestic skills that would make them useful additions to the family or institution that would take care of them.

Consequently, although Mom learned to read and was by the school's standards a good student, she didn't receive what teachers now would call a "good foundation" during her elementary school years. She wasn't encouraged to do things independently. Quite to the contrary, the nuns crimped any and all attempts at originality. I think they saw any deviations from the straight and narrow, either socially or religiously, as sins and, of course, sins had to be stamped out.

In line with this tradition, the nuns considered "work" and "duty" to be spiritually fortifying experiences. Even the youngest girls helped with kitchen chores and laundry. They washed their clothes, hung them in the courtyard to dry, and ironed them. They were taught to serve at teas and at church events for the speaking people who attended Sacred Heart Church in Oakland. These appearances were applauded by all concerned, with both the girls and the nuns being complimented for such "good" and "appropriate" behavior.

The nuns at the school in Oakland seemed to insist that their students learn to disregard the demands of their own bodies and purge all their sinful desires including a taste for candy, extra portions of food and shooting spitwads. Mom remembers them as very unsympathetic nurses who regarded sickness with suspicion and felt that any expressions of tenderness or concern encouraged malingering. They were particularly harsh with bed-wetters, and they seemed to consider menstruation a "curse" which the girls could overlook if they put their minds to it.

Shortly after her introduction into dormitory life, Mom was accused by one of the nuns of wetting her bed. She insists that it wasn't true, that someone else did it. It wouldn't be particularly unusual if she did, with Mom having gone from the protected surroundings of Gram's house in Glenn county to the dormitory and its unsympathetic nuns. Mom said the nuns became so angry when they found the soiled sheets that one of them seized Mom and forced her to her knees beside the bed, then grabbed her head and rubbed her face in it.

Such "training" was commonplace at the Oakland school. Gram admitted that Mom told her that she "didn't like the nuns at all" and particularly complained about having to wear the long black stockings required of all students. "Oh! and they were ugly! really ugly!" Gram conceded. Mom consistently called the nuns "—mean—and she said she "—hated them."

In part this "hatred" evolved from problems the girls faced as they approached puberty. Mom experienced the changes and traumas that beset all young girls while she was at the school. When she was 10, she lay in the infirmary, isolated from her friends, for over two weeks with the mumps. She began menstruating while at school; some of her older friends told her what was happening to her but she missed not having Gram to turn to when she needed her.

And Gram missed having Mom. "I always wanted to be such a good mother to Mildred," she remembered, "but it was hard with her so far away. I really felt that I was being denied something that was important to me." Later she told me that she did so many things for "you girls"—her three grand-daughters—because she hadn't been able to help Mom when she was going through these same adolescent crises.

In most instances, these "crises" were over before Gram found out about them. The school informed the parents about any serious illnesses or discipline problems, but otherwise proceeded with their impersonal—and rather unsympathetic—institutional care. Sick children were sent to the infirmary once the nuns determined that a real problem was involved. Mere headaches, cramps, upset stomachs or sore throats were considered nuisances that the children should ignore. Mom developed a noticeable fever during class one day and was sent to the infirmary to "rest." One of the nuns considered to be a "nurse" (I don't know how much actual medical training she had), examined Mom and prescribed a dose of medicine—aspirin perhaps, or possibly castor oil—and Mom curled up, alone in the small, bare-walled room, and went to sleep.

She awakened hours later. Through a little casement window she could see a sliver of moonlight. For a few minutes she sat on the edge of the infirmary cot, a blanket wrapped around her legs, blinking and trying to get her bearings. Her fever had diminished. She stood up, momentarily dizzy, but decided that she felt steady enough on her feet to return to the dormitory and her own bed.

Her eyes adjusted to the darkness enough to enable her to find the door. She twisted the knob on the door but it wouldn't open. Puzzled, she tried again, then realized that it was locked. She banged on it but nothing happened. *I'm locked in! I'm locked in!* she wanted to scream but she only could form the thoughts, not the words. The wind blew clouds across the moon and evil shapes seemed to form at the window. In a panic, Mom began to cry.

Lights blinked on in the corridor that ran outside the infirmary. Mom pounded on the door again, then backed away. Through the crack beneath it, she could see shadows of her classmates passing in the hallway. Two of them stopped and she banged as loudly as she could, but the shadows skipped away. None of the deaf students could hear her, and none of the nuns were around.

Frightened, frustrated and tired, Mom slumped back on the infirmary bed. *How long will they keep me in here? Won't anybody come to let me out!* The questions triggered a new round of sobs. Limp and exhausted, she curled up, her eyes on the door and on the moving shadows visible beneath it.

Finally either her teacher or the nun who acted as a nurse realized what had happened and opened the infirmary to release Mom. *They apologized and apologized*, she told me in sign. But apologies couldn't undo the harm that had been done. The occurrence served to validate her perception that the nuns were "mean" and didn't take a personal interest in the deaf children they were supposed to educate and supervise.

The girls, and the boys in the adjoining school building (the playgrounds were separated by a high brick wall), managed little moments of revenge. Not too long after the infirmary incident, the fire drill alarm awakened the teachers and they rushed through the dormitories to arouse the deaf students and lead them out into the courtyard. State law mandated that fire drills be held at private as well as public schools on a regular basis. All the students appeared at their place in line outside the building, but one of the nuns—Sister Rita (Mom described her as "older" and "meaner" than the rest)—was missing. Before any of the adults determined what they should do, three of the older boys "volunteered" to rush back into the building and "rescue" Sister Rita.

As Mom described the incident to me, Sister Rita was sound asleep. The boys hardly paused to bang on her door before rushing in to pull her out of bed. She squealed, mortified that any male should see her in her long night robe, then lit out after her "rescuers," who nimbly ducked out of reach. *Her face got big and turned purple!* Mom described in sign. For weeks after the "rescue," imitations of Sister Rita dominated the girls' after hours story sessions. *We laughed and laughed and laughed,* Mom admitted.

Gram's sense of loss, of the incompleteness of a relationship severed by the long school year, prompted her to organize her life to give Mom everything that she had missed while she was away. Although Mom's birthday officially was September 8, the Carrieres celebrated it on August 8, so she would be home. Mom did come home for two weeks at Christmas, and for a week at Easter; each occasion made special by cooking fancy meals, sewing, buying presents and making sure that nuts, candy, oranges and other special treats were available.

"Summer," Gram remembered, "meant Mildred would come home. I did everything that I could for her. I spent as much time with her as I possibly could. I wanted her to know that she was loved. I wanted her to understand that this was her home, and that we hadn't wanted to send her away, but had no other choice."

Apparently Mom understood this. As much as Gram spoiled her, she nevertheless looked forward to returning to Oakland and her friends each fall. Once, when Gram burst into tears as they were taking Mom to the train station, Mom signed to her *Don't cry. I am not unhappy. You shouldn't be unhappy either!* Despite the "mean" nuns, and the impersonal facilities, Mom developed a strong peer group identification with the school, her deaf friends and the "deaf world" in which they lived. She perceived that this world and the "hearing world" that Gram and Papa belonged to were mutually exclusive. Her school friends always would be strangers in Gram's and Papa's world and her parents could not cross into and become a part of the deaf world centered at the school.

Each world seems to have had built-in insulations. The nuns were so cloistered, and strict, that their young charges had virtually no contact with anyone or anything in the city of Oakland. The summers that Mom spent in Glenn were equally isolating, and Mom developed few contacts outside of the circle of relatives and friends that she had known since she was born. When any of us goes on a trip, whether skiing or shopping, a recreation trip to Disneyland or a business trip to Sacramento, Mom's first question when we return is, "Did you see any deaf people?" Her world consists of two islands—relatives and friends is one, the "deaf world" the other—and they protrude like solid, identifiable bastions through a flowing vastness of social and political concerns with which she has only superficial contact.

Occasionally this flowing vastness forces a change, as it did when the Catholic hierarchy decided to close the parochial school for the deaf in 1938. Mom, then 15, suddenly and through no fault of her own, faced an abrupt and potentially traumatic change of life style. Papa and Gram contacted the State-run School for the Deaf located in Berkeley (then a separate Bay Area town centered around the University of California, but now virtually an Oakland suburb), but they were overcrowded and could not enroll any new students until the following year. For the first time in nine years, Mom would have to spend the entire year at home.

But neither Gram nor Papa ever were satisfied to let things slide. Each, in his and her quiet way, was a "doer" and each believed in the old pioneer values of building a future by sacrificing something in the present. Instead of contenting themselves with a shrug and "we've-done-what-we-can, Mildred-will-have-to-stay-with-us-for-the-year . . ." they began looking for alternatives that would enable Mom to continue her schooling.

The most viable of these alternatives was offered by a friend of the Carrieres, a Mrs. Freeman, the teacher at the tiny Liberty School. Until the Second World War, schools throughout rural northern California were locally supported, rather then centralized, and one-room school-houses were the rule, not the exception. When Mrs. Freeman learned that Mom could not get into the State school in Berkeley, she suggested to Gram that "—you send Mildred over and let me work with her."

The offer appealed to Gram and Papa, even though the Liberty School was further from their farm than the school in Glenn. Children travel much further to school today, but the roads are paved and the Willows school system takes students to and from the outlying rural area. A number of Mom's cousins attended Liberty School, including most of her Aunt Zeta Taylor's nine children. Thus, though the educational process would be quite different, Mom would not be among strangers.

Transportation back and forth to school proved to be a problem. Gram and Papa determined that it was too far from the house for Mom to walk every day, and Papa wasn't sure he could leave work consistently to make the two trips a day. Perceiving this, Aunt Zeta and Uncle Carl offered to let Mom stay in their home during the week and return to Papa and Gram on weekends. "She can walk back and forth with my children," Aunt Zeta explained. "That way, nothing will happen to her, and she can help watch the younger ones."

The agreement was struck and Mom, for the first (and only) time in her life, moved into an environment that did not belong exclusively to either of her two separate worlds. It was, however, basically an extension of her life at home, for Aunt Zeta and her children, like most of Mom's relatives, had learned some sign and could communicate with her. As Mrs. Freeman's "special" student, Mom was cast in a role similar to that that she was used to at home. And Aunt Zeta, like Gram, bent over backwards to make sure that no one picked on or ridiculed Mom.

"The experience was good for her," Gram told me. In her straightforward, no-fear-of-contradiction way, Gram asserted that Aunt Zeta "was a saint on earth." Gram, I've learned, always has held in high regard anyone who has treated Mom with attention and respect. The arrangement "worked very well" but Mom looked forward eagerly to attending her new "deaf world" school in Berkeley the following year.

Mom's always been so malleable! I remember thinking after a conversation about her with Gram. Throughout Mom's life, the people around her—people she trusts—have arranged things for her. She seems to regard these arrangements as though they emerged from the same order of nature that puts leaves on the trees in spring and takes them away in the fall. Or rather, she regards as natural the facts that somebody does the arranging for her. Her complaisance seems to reflect the attitude that her parents, her daughters, her teachers, her cousins and even her in-laws, have keys that fit magically into the world's routines and she flows along with them unquestioningly. Dentists' appointments, vacation trips, money matters, even her own housecleaning appear and disappear like natural phenomena over which she exercises no control.

At the same time she is so detached, and so trusting, that these changes of events, these arrangements made about her life by others, seldom inhibit or frustrate her. Only occasionally does her drive for independence assert itself. She can become stubborn and moody and wage private little wars against what she perceives as unfair or oppressive circumstances. One of these little wars arose when she was at her final year at the State School for the Deaf.

There during her teenaged years, Mom "emerged" as a human being. She liked the school. As an educational institution, it made greater demands upon her concentration and intelligence. She worked very hard to complete reports and assignments. She wrestled with subjects such as science and history that the teacher-nuns at the Catholic school had skimmed across. She was the kind of student who, if told to read to page 30 in a book, would read to page 30 and close it, never questioning why she would stop there instead of on page 27 or continue to page 33 or 34.

Even more intriguing, however, was the school's social life. The students were carefully chaperoned and dating was not permitted, but girls and boys attended classes together and met in groups at a wide variety of social events. Mom literally "bloomed." Pictures of her at the time show a straight, full-figured, attractive young woman with a shy, slightly dimpled smile about to crinkle into laughter. She went to football and basketball games, on field trips and to movies shown in the school auditorium. She learned a variety of card games, including pinochle and whist. Here, even more than at the Catholic school, she was in her element, surrounded by friends who shared her handicap and awakened to all the possibilities that life within the school could offer.

When Mom describes the Catholic school, she instinctively brings up how "mean" the nuns were and the games that she and her companions played to get around that institution's rigid rules. But when she describes the State School, she evokes pictures of her friends and acquaintances and the things that they did together.

Unfortunately, school life, with all its excitements, companionship and adventures, was coming to an end. Once a student reached the semester of his or her nineteenth birthday, he or she no longer could continue to attend classes. Mom was 16 when she first enrolled, so actually she spent only three years in Berkeley, but they were three of the most important years of her life.

Looking back, I realize how lonesome Mother must have become after she returned to Willows after her final semester in Berkeley. For the first time since she could remember, she would be spending a summer without the anticipation of a new school year to beckon from the future. Her summers at home always had been very special times but now there were little brothers to share the attention and the uncertainties of life in a community that, though familiar to her, offered few opportunities. It must have seemed both arid and somewhat threatening.

Most people take for granted the identity that hearing and talking gives them. From the time that we are infants, we adjust and react, develop our roles, our personalities, on what we hear and say. Mother's deafness excluded her from that process. From the time that she was an infant, she was "different" and that differentness prevented her from fitting into the community's social life. Gram and Papa admitted that they constantly were on guard to make sure no one took advantage of her. Thus, though almost everyone in the area knew her and was fond of her, there were few dates or parties or social outings for the deaf girl.

At Berkeley, and before that at the Catholic school in Oakland, the situation had been different. The students there all had shared the same disability. They were like an emigrant community bound by the common bond of their language—signing—into a separate society of rich and poor, studious and athletic, extravert and wallflower. Within that microcosm, they were, relatively speaking, "normal." Only when they extended their boundaries and ventured into the community that surrounded them did they become different again.

In Willows, those boundaries pulled tightly around Mother. Instead of the school, the family became her special little world in which she could move unselfconsciously without feeling like an outsider. She spent a great deal of time with her brothers, with Gram and, I presume, alone.

Though their daughter no longer was a child, Gram and Papa maintained their awareness that she had special needs. Long before Mom reached her nineteenth birthday, they had determined that she should come back to Willows to live. Mom, I'm sure, accepted this. Nevertheless, she must have felt some misgivings. She liked the school and the people who attended it with her. It was "her" world and the people spoke "her" language. She felt comfortable among them; as much as she loved Gram and Papa, she missed the companionship, activities and social life when she was home.

While at Berkeley, Mom had spent a few weekends off-campus. The students were allowed to leave if they were picked up by a relative. Gram's sister Marie and her husband still lived near Oakland and took Mom to their home. Apparently while staying with them, she sometimes dated—perhaps going to a movie or some other event with a classmate who, like her, was staying with a relative in the area.

Through friends at school, and perhaps through some of these social outings, Mom met her first earnest suitor. He was tall and good-looking, a few years older than Mom; Gram and Papa identified him as a "city boy" which is not, in Glenn County, a compliment. Like Mom, he had attended the State school. He and she corresponded after she returned to Willows and on at least one occasion he came to the Carriere's house to visit her.

In the meantime, Mom made several trips to Oakland. Gram and Papa arranged for her to stay with some relatives in the area. During these visits, Mom got together with a number of old school friends and went out with the "city boy." That Gram and Papa assented to these arrangements is, I think, a testimony to their cooperativeness and willingness to let Mom make some choices. They realized that she missed the school and wanted to continue her friendships with her classmates.

But there in Oakland something happened, something that hurt Gram so much that she scarcely ever mentioned those trips to Oakland when I was young. For a long time I thought that Mom had broken a curfew or failed to obey some rule at the relatives' house. But when I pressed Gram for details she became upset. She didn't want to talk about Mom's behavior, Mom's suitor, or what had happened in Oakland. But finally, under my coaxing, she relented.

It wasn't anything that Mom had done, she explained, but the way Mom was! The relatives in Oakland liked Mom very much and certainly didn't want to hurt her feelings. But there were "problems." They couldn't communicate with her. Without saying it directly, they intimated that Mom was an embarrassment to them. They felt they couldn't have their friends over while she was visiting them. Telling Gram and Papa about it made them feel as awkward and uncomfortable as Mom's presence in their home made them feel. They alternately justified what they were doing and apologized for finding it necessary. They even acknowledged their own limitations. But that didn't change the situation. Quite simply, they couldn't cope with having a deaf-mute living with them.

Gram was shocked. She and Papa immediately agreed not to send Mom again. I think it was the first time that anyone close to Gram had pierced the protective covering that she had woven to enclose my mother. She had tried, almost single-handedly, to make mother "normal." All of a sudden that wasn't enough.

Every person with a physical handicap encounters that kind of rejection at some point or another. For the deaf, it is particularly aggravating. Not only does their disability separate them from conversational interchange, it makes them seem less capable mentally than they really are. Attempting to cope with this difficulty embarrasses many non-deaf people. They look away when two deaf people are signing. They squirm and blush when a deaf person asks them a question, even when they understand what the gestures mean. They reply self-consciously, as though afraid someone will laugh if they are seen talking with their hands. Or they will become brusk and imperative, grab things or physically shove the deaf person around.

The relatives in Oakland reacted in some of these ways. They liked Mom but they simply couldn't cope with the social problems that they felt it caused them.

Mom wasn't told why she couldn't go back to Oakland. She now was 22 or 23, slim and attractive and neatly groomed, with a bright smile and flashing eyes. She was corresponding with her suitor and he was urging her to make another Bay Area visit. Finally Gram had to tell her that it couldn't be arranged.

I don't know what effect this restriction had on the budding romance. Gram remembers that Mom was upset and didn't understand why she was being thwarted. Mom had grown up assuming that the details of her life would be arranged for her, so perhaps she only regarded it as a puzzling and temporary setback. Soon after this, she did begin mentioning that she and her suitor were considering getting married.

Gram and Papa tactfully circumvented any rash moves. Since Mom and her suitor were not yet formally engaged, it was not necessary to start discussing wedding plans. They asked Mom to wait at least a year in order to know her prospective husband better, and to meet and discuss the proposed match with his parents. After that, Gram promised, there would be a wedding—a big one, with a huge wedding cake, gifts, a hall filled with people, a honeymoon. There would be new dresses and new shoes, a traveling outfit, all the things that a bride would need to make the ceremony a success.

Papa, like many men of his generation, was firm and practical. If the decision to oppose the marriage was his (which at least in part it was), he left it to Gram to do the convincing. There was no confrontation, only a lengthy—but apparently a largely one-sided—conversation. And Mother, given the details of the wedding, was easy to convince. She liked pretty things and she liked to be fussed over. Her consent was consistent with her personality.

I've mentioned that neither Gram nor Papa were particularly impressed by their prospective son-in-law. Despite his good looks, he was emotional and, I gather, somewhat brusque. Although they didn't want to slam the door on the match, or oppose Mom if she really did want to marry, they were quite certain in their own minds that this was not the right man for their daughter.

It is difficult to assess just how much of Gram's and Papa's protectiveness was due to my mother's deafness and how much of it was a natural reflection of their own backgrounds and beliefs. Neither the Second World War nor the surge of new residents to California that followed it immediately affected the Willows-Glenn area. Almost everyone in that farming community knew everyone else—farming families tended to be large, and provincial; stay-at-home children married their neighbors' children or high school classmates, and farms and businesses were expanded or re-divided to accommodate the new unions. The thought of Mother marrying an outsider, who would take her away to live in the city, obviously disturbed Gram and Papa. Quite possibly they would have objected to such a match even if Mother had not been deaf.

Like many disappointed lovers before and since, Mom's intended reacted angrily. He dashed off a note threatening to burn Papa's farm down if mother didn't marry him. Gram responded by writing to the young man's sister, whom my mother apparently knew, and the sister wrote back explaining that her brother had emotional problems. With that, whatever doubts that Gram and Papa might have had about intervening in the marriage disappeared.

CHAPTER IV

By 1946 the suitor from Oakland had dropped out of my mother's life. She seemed to accept her role within the family, within the town and among the people who knew her and treated her as a very special, if handicapped and "different," individual. A flow of relatives moved in and out of the house beside the levee. There were family get-togethers every Sunday, either at Gram's and Papa's house or at one of the other relatives. Mom did some of the baking and took part in work around the house, the farm, and in family celebrations and outings.

Gram and Papa did everything they could to make Mother feel wanted and important. They looked for opportunities that would enable her to expand her personal and social life. One of these opportunities involved Henry Enos, who as a young boy several years before had traveled back and forth to Berkeley on the train with her.

My Dad, as a teenager, bore little resemblance to the confused little crybaby that mother had escorted on the train. Snapshots show him as handsome, cocky "Jock Studley," halfback on the school football team, star basketball guard and heads-up infielder. He was a meticulous dresser who took more pains about his appearance than he did about his grades in school. He spent his summers on his father's farm. Even then he was a hard worker, always out to prove that he could do anything that any other hand could do.

I suppose, from the time that they were small children, Mom and Dad were destined to marry each other. They had so much in common, each being the first-born, each being deaf, each having grown up on a farm in Glenn County. While they were in Berkeley, they'd had little to share; Mom, being five years older, had separate interests and friends. But I imagine that they acknowledged each other as "someone from back home" when they ran across each other in hallways or on the school grounds before or after class.

The similarities do not extend all the way back through their childhood, however. My father's parents, Frank ("Avo"—the Portuguese word for grandfather) and Elsie Enos, did not protect their son the way that Gram and Papa Carriere protected my mother. Their love for him and concern for his well-being were tempered by Old World values. Avo, in particular, had a hard time dealing with the fact that his first-born could not hear or speak. Consequently throughout his life, Dad bucked what he has considered to be unfair odds in order to prove himself.

Like many Sacramento Valley farmers, the Enoses are of Portuguese descent. Avo's parents first came to California from the Azores Islands

around the turn of the century. Avo was born in Santa Clara, then a
sleepy farming town surrounded by prune orchards and alfalfa fields. A
few years later, his parents moved to a farm on the West side near
Willows. Avo attended a little country school, Kanawha School, one of
three then located on Country Road D (the other two were Cherokee and
Liberty, the one that Mom entered when she lived with her Aunt Zeta in
1937) but he only stayed through the fifth grade. By then he was old
enough and big enough to be useful on the farm, and his parents saw no
reason for him to continue.

I remember asking him about Kanawha School and his response was
an immediate, "Ah! You should have seen me! Boy, I was the best
baseball player! When I'd come up to bat, everybody'd shout, Back up!
Back up! Frank's coming up!" I laughed and he jumped to his feet. "No!
No!" he insisted, "I'm not kidding! I could really hit that ball! I loved
baseball! I really loved it!"

Despite such Americanizations, Avo's ties to the Azores remained
strong. When he was 23, he and his brother Manuel sailed to Portugal to
visit the Shrine of the Lady of Fatima, and on their return stopped in the
Azores to stay with relatives. Their mother engineered the trip. Some
months before, Avo and Manuel had contracted influenza. A week of high
fever and vomiting prompted their mother to pray for their recovery. She
promised the Holy Gost that she would send them to the Old Country "to
get the Crown" if they got well. When the boys' fever broke and they
recovered, she insisted that they keep her end of the bargain. Despite the
cost, the two young men boarded an East-bound passenger train for the
3,000- mile trip to New York, then a ship for the 14-day ocean crossing to
Lisbon.

Good-looking, successful, even wealthy by Azores' standards and confident, Avo made his presence on the islands known. One day at a
bullfight he boldly struck a conversation with a dark-haired, dark-eyed
teenager named Elsie Nunes. She promptly fell in love with this "handsome American" who soon was going to return to his native California. A
month later they were married, and two days after the ceremony Elsie
Nunes Enos was on a boat heading for the United States.

"He robbed me!" Grandma Enos laughed as she told me about her age
and the whirlwind courtship.

"You knew him less than a month before you married him?" I teased
her.

"Well . . ." her eyes sparkled but her voice was under control, steady
and serious ". . . I knew he was a good man. You could tell. And I could
have stayed in the Old Country and married a man who wasn't good. So I
said yes."

In many ways, she was a perfect complement to Avo—accepting where
he was aggressive, appreciative and giving where he was determined and

ambitious. There was little of modern America in the roles that they brought to their marriage. Rural California was far removed from the flapper era depicted in John Barrymore and George Raft movies, and the sturdy Azores farmers showed little inclination to alter their views about what relationships between men and women should be like.

Not that Grandma Enos ever strove for the kind of independence now typified by women's liberation movements. She had grown up expecting to be a housewife and mother; the fertile Sacramento Valley, flat as far as the eye could see, the size of Avo's holdings and the determination and energy he threw into managing them and making his crops grow, provided her with more opportunities—and comforts—than her childhood in the Azores ever had promised.

For the first years of their marriage, Avo and his "child bride" lived with his parents on the farm north of Willows. In order to acquire a place of his own, Avo sold his share of the family's dairy herd to his brothers. With the money from this transaction he bought a little "ranch" and put a house on it. Even as a young man, he had a knack for business—the right purchase, the right crop, the right trade—and a capacity to work from dawn to dusk day after day, week after week, year after year. Intellectually, he reduced everything to basic simplicities—rights and wrongs, bargains which were sacred trusts, actions which included putting his fist down and saying *No!* and meaning *No!* till Hell froze over. More than once, his grandchildren, including me, have accused him of tunnel vision and he, in turn, has only snorted and viewed us as wafflers who can't make up their minds.

Devoutly Catholic, his beliefs are so firm and unflinching they seem almost Medieval, Avo made bargains with God . . . and kept them. He gave both time and money to Saint Monica's, the parish church in Willows. I suspect that, in doing so, he was fulfilling a promise or promises made to God when he was a struggling young farmer. In my mind's eye, I can picture him saying, "Please, Father, let these crops be successful this year and I will do such-and-such for Your church. . . ." Then, God having kept His part of the bargain, Avo most certainly would keep his. A handshake to him was a solemn vow. Mitigating factors were not even a consideration.

An Old World farmer's pride and joy is his sons. They are a reason for living, working, achieving. They define his manhood, give him a place in the world, and he, in turn, gives them identity by being a solid and prosperous provider. Thus, when Grandma Enos announced that she was pregnant, Avo's chest swelled. In typical Old World fashion, he hoped for a son—and he was not disappointed.

Not at first, at least. Grandma became sick midway through her pregnancy and the baby—my father—weighed only three pounds when he was born. "He was so tiny," Grandma Enos recalls, "that he could fit into a shoe box." He seemed so frail that both she and Avo feared for his life. Grandma couldn't find any baby clothing small enough to fit him so she dressed him in doll clothes. She held him, nursed him, rocked him, sang to him. Each ounce that he gained evoked cries of delight. Both she and Avo wanted so much for him to gain strength and grow that I'm sure they prayed for him constantly. I feel certain that Avo made promises to God and kept those promises after my father finally began to grow.

But in those petitions—and the granting of them—apparently no guarantees of perfectability were struck. As far as his parents were concerned, Dad was a normal child. Despite his slow start, he developed as all babies develop. He learned to crawl, to feed himself, to complain when his diapers were wet and eventually, to walk.

But he couldn't hear. The realization came slowly to Grandma Enos. At first she attributed his deafness to his age—he was developing slowly, she told herself. Sometimes, when he seemed to respond, she told herself that he was going to be all right. After all, he was an active child, energetic, strong-willed—and like many first-born a bit spoiled and catered to by a doting mother. She watched him, talked to him, tested him by calling him or speaking to him when he wasn't looking. He didn't react to these tests, nor did he play with toys. Gradually she became convinced that his deafness was real, not something she was imagining.

But Avo wouldn't hear of it. He knew what young boys were like— he'd been one himself. "He's just stubborn," he told Grandma. "He hears what he wants to hear and ignores the rest." Less worry and a few more solid whacks across the butt were what he needed.

But even Avo, with all his strong will and determination, couldn't postpone the truth forever. Father now was three years old and though alert and physically active he still wasn't learning to talk. Avo agreed that there was "—some kind of problem—" and told Grandma, "We'll take him to a good doctor—he can cure it."

Once again Avo was thwarted. The drive 45 miles across the valley to a doctor in Chico, a small commercial hub surrounded by almond orchards and walnut trees, only confirmed what Grandma had suspected. Father was deaf. "How can we get him fixed?" Avo demanded. The doctor tried to explain that the human body wasn't a tractor or harvester that could be repaired with wrenches and a screwdriver but Avo was insistent. Surely there's something that can be done! The doctor shrugged. Little was then known about deafness: the ear, like the eye, was a delicate mechanism, the doctor explained; sometimes people were born deaf or blind, others lost their sight and hearing gradually. He wasn't a specialist; as far as he could determine, the problem was a permanent, rather than a temporary condition. He did, however, give Avo and Grandma the name of another doctor in Sacramento.

Avo and Grandma weren't content merely to accept father's condition as an act of fate from which there could be no recourse. They took Father to Sacramento and when the doctor there couldn't provide any remedies or alternatives, they contacted a specialist in San Francisco. At each step along the way, each examination and diagnosis, Avo determinedly asked for cures. Couldn't you operate on him? Maybe there's something that needs to come out? Maybe something needs to be reconnected? And the doctors, as puzzled about the causes of deafness as he was, could only say No, it's not within our range of skills, there's nothing we can do.

Finally the doctor in San Francisco put his arm around Avo's shoulder and told him, "Frank, you're wasting your time. There's nothing that the medical profession can do for your son. He has an ear like glass. He'll never be able to hear."

Avo was not used to accepting defeat but he was a realist and knew when he had reached the limits of his determination. It was God's will and there wasn't anything that he could do about it. Knowing Avo, I feel sure that he prayed that Dad be given the ability to hear. And, bargain-keeper that he was, I'm sure that whatever he had promised to do for God if his prayers were answered went undone.

Avo never quite recovered from his disappointment. He could say, always, very sincerely and without fear of contradiction, that he loved my father. But a gulf developed between them—a gulf caused by the fact that my father was deaf. A subtle sort of rejection seemed to take place, gradual but definite. Father was not the son that Avo wanted. The boy was lively and feisty and ornery and stubborn—all qualities that could recommend a boy to his Portuguese father—but he also was incomplete, a piece of damaged merchandise as it were. Not that Avo ever consciously thought of Father that way, but that seemed to be his reactions. It became more evident after my father was grown and rearing a family of his own and Avo, instead of entrusting the bulk of the farm business to Dad, handed it instead to my Uncle John, who was seven years younger than Dad.

It is difficult, always, to separate the effects of a disability like deafness from normal emotional patterns that might shape, or distort, an individual's personality. There is a tendency to attribute everything to the handicap: Oh! it's because he's deaf that he's so ornery . . .! or, she's deaf, that's why she is so very shy. Or, of course he's moody! He's deaf, you know! I'm sure that many things that my father did—and perhaps didn't do— were blamed on his disability, even though he came by his zest and energy honestly. Avo once admitted, "He was too much like me, the little rascal!"

Imagine, if you can, this healthy, spirited farm boy with keen eyesight and quick reactions growing up without words. And think about your own pre-school years which, for most children, are times of great imaginary happenings. Father was cut off from this world. He had a human mind and animal's instincts; his brain and consequently his imagination were completely untrained. He like doing things with his hands. He liked throwing rocks. He liked pounding things. He learned to milk the cows and do other chores and swaggered proudly when he was rewarded for a job well done.

But he was cut off from his parents. He couldn't tell them what he felt or thought and they couldn't talk to him except through a rudimentary sign language that they had developed. Sign Language is difficult for many to learn, but imagine how Grandma Enos felt when she realized not only did she have to learn English (having been in this country a few years) she had to learn to speak to her son in a different language altogether. He was easily—and often—frustrated by his inability to convey his discoveries, immediacies, questions, needs. There were too few outlets for those enthusiasms and the intelligence building up inside him. And Avo and Grandma Enos, instead of being over-protective as Gram and Papa Carriere had been with Mother, often treated him too abruptly, as though he were much younger than he actually was.

He loved to play with gravel. And he liked being around Avo. One day a Willows car dealer by the name of Johnson came to the ranch to try to sell Avo a car. As I've said, Avo was a shrewd bargainer—he knew what questions to ask and what prices to pay— and the two got into a detailed discussion about the merits of the vehicles Mr. Johnson was offering. Since he couldn't hear what was going on, Dad couldn't take part in the discussion in even a fringe way, so he settled himself on the gravel driveway while the two men tried to out-fox each other.

For some reason, Mr. Johnson's shoes attracted Dad. He crawled over to investigate them. As always, he had a handful of gravel; on impulse he poured it on one of the salesman's glistening black oxfords. Then another handful. Mr. Johnson's shoes gradually disappeared beneath twin-coned mountains of gravel and sand. Just as the two men struck a bargain, the salesman looked down and, according to Avo "looked momentarily shock-ed, then he burst out laughing. For a minute he must have thought that he'd hit quicksand and was sinking into the driveway!"

Enclosed as he was in his wordless, silent world, Dad never quite knew how to react to the sudden bursts of movement that characterized Avo's reactions to one kind of stunt or another. Another visitor to the ranch also got the sand and gravel treatment. Avo remembers him as A. J. Lewis, a local merchant who, like many men in the 30's, wore a stylish felt-brimmed hat.

Invited into the house, Lewis removed his hat and placed it on an end table. Always the curious one, Dad ambled in to inspect the visitor, then—as he often did—he disappeared from view. No one saw him reappear beside the end table, look back from the hat to his fists, each clutching a load of precious gravel, look back at the hat and carefully line the brim with sand and small stones.

His business concluded, Lewis stood up, reached for his hat and turned to make a final remark to Avo. The sand and gravel that Dad had poured on the hat brim cascaded down Lewis's face, into his collar and onto his shirt. He sputtered, barely able to control his tongue—apparently, he thought Avo had played a practical joke on him.

"Oh!" To this day, Avo lifts and clenches his fist when he retells the incident, "I was so damned mad! I tell you, I could have killed your father!"

Phrases like that typified Avo's reactions to his deaf son. Avo was strict and firm and saw everything as either black or white. He didn't have time for innuendoes, second guessing or arbitration. And Dad, admittedly, was a tease and often pushed his luck farther than Avo would let it go.

But Dad's responses to his parents weren't always good-natured. A pattern of frustration that has extended throughout his adult life had its roots in those pre-school years. He comprehended, wanted and needed so much more than he could express. Often, unable to get a point across, he would quiver with a frustration that bordered on rage. Or, thwarted, he would seek outlet in a physical act and express himself with his hands, his legs, his muscles.

One day Grandma Enos refused to let him in the house. She was mopping the floors and didn't want him tracking mud or dirt inside. Dad needed something—something that at the time seemed very important to him—and he tried to explain what it was. Again Grandma Enos shooed him away. The answer was no; she wasn't going to stop what she was doing; as far as she was concerned, he could just go about his business until the floors were dry.

Unable to vocalize his frustration—or even frame words into thoughts within his own mind—Dad stomped across the yard. I can picture him kicking rocks, or picking them up and throwing them at a tree or the dog or the barn, his emotions aswirl, his frustration seeking some outlet, some focus for its intensity.

His path led him to the chicken pen. Instinctively he grabbed a stick and went after the chickens, intent on some kind of revenge, swatting and eventually isolating one of them and dragging it outside the pen, where he swatted it again.

The bird teetered giddily and Dad grabbed it around the neck, on impulse heading for the creek, where apparently he intended to drown it. Avo, coming across the field, saw him and started after him. As Avo described the incident, Dad would drop the groggy chicken everytime it tried to escape and whack it on the head with his stick until it keeled over, then, half-carrying and half-dragging it, head towards the creek again.

He repeated the process half-a-dozen times. Avo slowed down, intent on sneaking up on his son, who he knew couldn't hear and probably wouldn't notice him.

But for some reason, Dad looked up just before Avo got to him. One glimpse of Avo's face was all that Dad needed—he dropped the chicken and took off running, Avo behind him, shouting and cursing as they zigzagged through clumps of brush and thistles. Dad, nimble and athletic despite his short legs, was more than a match for his father but endurance eventually won out and Avo cornered and grabbed him.

"Damn that kid! Damn him! Oh, I was so mad!" Avo remembered. "Right there I took my belt off and I beat the shit out of him!"

Such punishments may have kept Dad in line but they did little to alleviate his frustrations. Avo and Grandma Enos knew that Glenn County's rural schools could do little to educate him. I think that they assumed that they would keep him home, where he could do some work on the farm and would be loved and cared for. But, as it turned out, father was not the only deaf child of Portuguese descent in the North Valley.

The Portuguese families tended to be very clannish. They all had strong Old Country ties, and most of them had immigrated to the United States at about the same time. The preservation of their old values, particularly those centered around religious and social events, enlarged their world geographically. From Sacramento to Redding, Reno to San Jose, they met for weddings, dances and festivals; they borrowed from each other, traded land, livestock and seed, compared notes on visits back to the Islands and stuffed each other with linguicia, bread, cheese and home-made wine. I doubt that any family of Portuguese descent in the Valley was unknown to the others; unlike settlers and homesteaders who came West from other parts of the United States, they seemed to operate from within a much larger kin-help network. To be Portuguese meant that one belonged to a complex, quite large and multi-faceted family.

Through this structure, and the social intercourse that it provided, Avo and Grandma Enos learned that a Portuguese family in Chico, the Azevedos, had deaf children. They talked to this family and learned that their children attended the State School for the Deaf in Berkeley. Apparently the Azevedos advised, or at least suggested, that Avo and Grandma Enos send Father there. They even told them that it could be arranged for their children and Henry to ride the train to Berkeley together.

Always the practical, hard-bargaining—but astute—dairy owner and farmer that he was, Avo balanced the pros and cons. He talked to Grandma and to his business contemporaries. He decided it would be to Father's advantage to go to school in Berkeley. Grandma, though sentimentally opposed to the idea, agreed that her son needed to learn the things that the school could provide. They made all the arrangements for Father to enroll and told him about it. Immediately he began to cry. *NO!* he told them *I don't want to go away! I want to stay here with you!*

"It was like a pin in my heart, it hurt so bad!" Grandma Enos barely could face parting with her son. She was under pressure from relatives and neighbors to keep him at home and rear him herself. In 1935, that would have been the conventional thing to do. But Grandma had fiber; she was tough and stubborn. Good person that she was, she could grab herself by the scruff of the neck and tell herself, "All right woman, cry for him if you must, but do what is best for him." Best, in their son's case, was the State School. Both she and Avo became convinced of that.

Looking back, I wonder just what they expected from the School for the Deaf? Certainly they regarded it as more than a caretaking institution, for they expected that Father would learn to write and read there. Not a great deal was understood about the psychology of those who were born deaf in the 30's, and what was known wasn't available to people in isolated parts of the Sacramento Valley. When I asked her about it, Grandma shrugged. "We had faith," she said simply. Then, "What else could we do? He was such a bright boy. He needed the opportunity."

However, Father didn't perceive it as an opportunity. He didn't want to leave the farm. Unlike Mother, he didn't react with open-armed amazement that there was a whole world of people like him. From the beginning, he rebelled against identifying himself as deaf. Being sent away from the ranch, and his mother and father, into a strange and distant city and a school with strict teachers and stricter rules was, to him, a punishment. *You do it because I can't hear and talk like you do* I can picture him signing. And Grandma Enos, barely able to restrain her tears, nods *yes*.

How much of what they felt about their son were Avo and Grandma Enos able to convey to him? Denied the use of language, they had to resort to the simplest communications—signs, hugs, tears. I gather from the way that he describes his boyhood, my father constantly was aware that his deafness created problems for others. Avo openly stated, then and long after Dad was grown and married, that Dad was a torment, a cross to bear.

Now, because of his deafness, Dad was being sent to a special school. Did he feel rejected? Unloved? Many deaf people are confused by their feelings and don't know how to react to them or describe them. They sense quite keenly that they are being excluded because of their handicap. They become psychologically as well as physically isolated. Feelings of inferiority and low self-esteem are common. Because they have difficulty in expressing complex feelings, they often are treated as though they lack those feelings. They are ignored, or choices are taken away from them. They are regarded as "slow," or deficient, or even retarded.

Fortunately, neither of my parents had to cope with extremes like those. But Father, at six, a country boy who'd hardly been away from home except to visit relatives, had to face a sudden change of environment. That further singled him out as "different" and he didn't want to be different. He wanted to be his father's pride-and-joy, his heir—as the first-born in any Portuguese family would want to be. And as well as he finally accommodated to the necessity of going to school and learning to cope with his handicap, he bristled whenever he was treated as less than an equal by family, contemporaries or friends.

The school sent Grandma Enos a list of the clothing Father would need for the school year. Avo, she remembers, insisted that they buy the best clothes that they could afford. The entire wardrobe—shirts, shoes, coat, trousers, sweaters, neckties, etc.—cost almost $100!

"Oh! He looked like such a little man!" Even now the memory of him standing stiff and unhappy as she fussed over him brings tears to Grandma Enos' eyes. She described his traveling clothes for that trip and later trips that he made by train. "He had gray wool short pants with suspenders, a white shirt, knee-high socks, black patent shoes and a gray wool cap to go with it all. Ah! he was such a handsome, unhappy little fellow!"

The trip to Berkeley to deliver Father to the school was a funereal affair. Avo, stiff and incommunicative, drove and Grandma alternately fussed over her confused and unhappy son, prayed, then tried to show him all the exciting new sights visible through the car windows. When they stopped in front of the school, a small but formidable structure, very institutional in its plain, fortress-like exterior, Grandma wanted to "turn around and go back home." But Avo, always a man of his word, shook his head. They'd made their decision, they were going to stick by it.

The administrators and teachers at the school were very "professional, very kind" Grandma Enos remembers. Nevertheless, turning her only child over to them was "like selling him into slavery." The moment made an indelible impression upon her. As she described it, *"Come,* one of the teachers beckoned to Henry. They took him into a room. They showed him some objects and showed him how to pick out colors that were exactly alike. We watched him through a one-way mirror. He was all bleary-eyed but very intent on the project. The teacher came over to us. Why don't you go?' she suggested. I looked at Avo—I didn't want to go, I didn't want to leave him there—but Avo nodded. We walked away, I couldn't keep myself from crying. I hurt all over inside."

The trip back to Willows took "a lifetime." Even Avo broke down. As Grandma Enos remembered it, "We'd drive a few miles, then he couldn't see any longer and we'd stop and cry. I thought we'd never get home."

Looking back, I'm surprised that the Enoses kept Dad in the State School throughout his grammar school years. Grandma described that first year that he was gone: "I cried at everything. I'd see his clothes, I'd cry. I'd see his bed, I couldn't help it, I'd cry. The whole ranch seemed empty without him. I felt like a barren woman."

Over and over Grandma's friends would tell her how cruel she was to have sent her little boy so far away. "You should raise him yourself!" "I

think it's terrible! Him down there away from his family and all alone!"
"What if something happens to him? Here you could look after him. He'd
have a good home!"

But the Enoses weren't to be dissuaded. Grandma Enos once told me,
"In my heart I knew it was the best place for him. He needed to learn his
language and I knew that I couldn't teach him myself." And Avo, having
set his course, wouldn't deviate from it, even though Father insisted that
he hated Berkeley and wanted to stay on the ranch.

The Carrieres remember seeing Dad standing forlornly between Avo
and Grandma Enos on the railroad platform waiting for the train. And
Mom, who was of course older than Dad, had adjusted to school and
enjoyed the peer group companionship, once told her parents that the
Enos boy sniveled and cried all the way to Berkeley. And John, Dad's
younger brother, remembered, "He'd cry when he had to leave. It was
tough on him because he couldn't express his emotions or feelings. He
couldn't say in words anything that meant anything emotionally; hence
the tears."

If adjusting to school life presented difficulties to Father, it was, at
times, even more difficult for Grandma Enos. Husband, home and children were her entire life and she felt deprived because she couldn't share
many of her important events in her son's life. His boyhood virtually was
split in two and, although he spent his summers on the ranch, he was in
Berkeley when he had the measles, when he received communion, when
he lost his first tooth—all the little events that parents remember and
use as guideposts to record their children's development and growth.

The low point came when Father caught pneumonia. The school notified Avo and Grandma Enos that their son was in "serious" condition.
Avo had no one to help him at the dairy and he couldn't leave the cows
unmilked, so he got up before dawn and took care of them, then he and
Grandma jumped into their car and drove down to Berkeley. Although
many of northern California roads were paved—and even bore the desig-
nations "highways"— those that linked rural Glenn County with the Bay
Area wound from one small town to another along narrow two-lane strips
of asphalt obstructed by farm vehicles, residential slow-downs and stop
signs. The trip took over five hours and Avo could only stay with his son
until time to make the return trip home to do the evening milking.

Again Grandma Enos felt pins in her heart. They repeated the trip the
next day, and the day after that. Gradually Father got better and by the
end of the week he was out of danger. But, to Grandma Enos, he
"—seemed so tiny and so lonesome and so far away." Her determination
to keep him in the School for the Deaf wavered but Avo, stubborn and
certain of his convictions, prevailed and Father remained at Berkeley. It
really was the best thing for him.

Now, Father no longer was an only child. His brother John was born in

March, 1937. For several years, immediately before and right after John's birth, Avo had been promising Grandma Enos a trip back to the Azores. Finally, he arranged for his brothers to oversee the dairy and soon after Dad returned home from Berkeley in the summer of 1936 he and Grandma packed their trunks for a month-long stay in the "Old Country."

A week or so before they were to catch the train East, little John got sick. The illness was serious enough to worry Avo. He drove to St. Monica's, lit prayer candles and promised God that he would distribute food to the poor in the Azores if God would let John get well.

Almost immediately, John's fever diminished. Avo returned to St. Monica's to thank God and reaffirm his vow. Then he bundled his wife and two sons onto the train. Three days later they were on a ship steaming towards the Azores.

In the Portuguese-owned islands, Avo made good on his promise. He bought a beef and had it butchered. The butcher and his assistant "put all this meat on a cart, like the carts you see comin' across the prairies in the olden days," he told me. They yoked an ox to the cart and Avo, helped by Dad and several of his wife's relatives, headed along the cobbled streets of Grandma Enos' hometown.

"We'd take a fig leaf and set the meat on it," Avo explained. "Then we'd put another leaf over the top and the boys would knock on each door and give the meat to the person who lived there." While Avo was directing traffic from the seat of the ox-cart, one of Grandma Enos' uncles pulled Dad aside and showed him how to rub his fingers together in the universal sign for money, Dad, always a "sharp little rascal" (to quote Avo), caught on quickly. He'd run up to a door, the gift of beef in hand, hand the resident the meat and rub his fingers together to indicate *money!*

When the party got back to the house where Dad and Avo were staying, Avo looked at Dad and saw that he had a pocket stuffed full of money.

"Oh my God!" Avo boomed. "I could have killed him! I was so embarrassed!" He clapped his hands together and shook his head. "Well, it wasn't Henry's fault, really. It was the uncle's fault. That uncle, I could've just . . . Boy! We had a big argument over that!"

"What did you do with the money?" I wanted to know.

Avo shrugged. "I didn't know how much people had given. There was no way to keep track of it. We couldn't give it back, so we gave it to the Church. It was just a lesson that Henry had to learn. But for me it was awfully embarrassing!"

According to Avo, Dad was very popular in the Azores. That assertion surprised me, for Dad never has spoken fondly of his experiences there and once told me that he never wanted to go back, even to visit. "He made many friends," Avo insisted, and added that the people were fascinated by him and his deafness and his ability to communicate in sign.

Dad's companion on the Islands was his great-uncle. They used to walk together. This uncle was patient and attentive and tried to understand Dad's sign language communications. One morning they left a gathering in a park to stroll to a little corner baker and buy some sweet bread. As they returned, munching the rolls and conversing in their make-shift language, some people from the village began to follow them.

"When they got back to the park where I was waiting," Avo remembered, "I looked up. Hey! What's going on?" I shouted. There must have been thirty people following Henry and that uncle. They seemed to be astonished by the way he was talking with his hands. It was like he was the Pied Piper!"

They returned to Willows for the remainder of the summer and Dad returned to Berkeley to school in the fall. As always, he was fussy and resentful and, as Avo put it "made a scene." Gradually, however, he acclimatized to life in Berkeley and became more well established within his peer group. It changed his perceptions and, to some extent, his personality. He was becoming more independent and reflected peer group values and pressures. At 11, Grandma Enos remembers, he stopped milking the cows, as he eloquently demonstrated in sign language, their tails "have shit on them!"

If those first years in school worked hardships upon the homesick boy who never before had been confined to an indoor routine of books, classrooms and supervised meals, the later ones found him rising into peer group prominence. He was a good athlete and a natty dresser. He made numerous friends and loved being photographed with them. Like many teenagers of his era, he shrugged his shoulders at studying and didn't make very good grades. A school administrator later told Papa Carriere, "That Enos boy only uses his head to keep his ears apart."

Snapshots taken while he was in school confirm that he was a halfback on the football team. By his own admission, he was nothing short of an All-American. He often, he will tell you, cut between blockers to gallop down the sidelines for a touchdown. He caught passes thrown high over his head and, on defense, was a ferocious tackler. His team did, in fact, compete against a number of small, denominational high schools in the Oakland-Berkeley area, and I have no reason to believe that Dad wasn't one of the league's better performers. Some of his gridiron exploits, however, might have become exaggerated in the telling and retelling of them. In my family, such things have been known to happen.

Dad's younger brother John remembered making a trip to the California School for the Deaf during one of Dad's last two or three years there. Dad was out of action at the time, having dislocated his shoulder during a football game. Avo, with John, then about ten or eleven years old, in tow, was given a tour of the campus. "I remember we talked to Henry's coach, and the vice-president of the school. They both had good things to say about Dad, especially concerning athletics."

"But Henry acted kind of embarrassed. I guess he didn't want his Dad and brother to see him with his arm in a sling. He went into a long explanation about how he had fallen the wrong way when he had been tackled. He showed us *I should have done this, I should have fallen this way.* . . .

"He was really macho. I guess he equated being hurt with having failed."

Baseball, not football, probably was Dad's best game. Some of the men who played with and against him in the Willows area remember that scouts from a number of professional teams took an interest in him. The Second World War had just ended and towns throughout the country were hooking up with Major League farm systems. Even Willows, with less than 2,000 people, entered a franchise in the Class D Far West League for a couple of seasons. Apparently Dad never actually was offered a contract, and I don't know what affect his being deaf may have contributed to his being by-passed by professional baseball, but he was good enough to have merited consideration.

Dad, like Avo, saw no reason to be shy when it came to athletic accomplishments. The high point of his athletic career at the School for the Deaf came when they hosted a highly favored Livermore High School baseball team. Each club scored early; at the end of regulation time (seven innings), the score was tied 2–2. It was getting dark and the umpires notified both benches that the game would be called if neither team scored in the ninth inning. Livermore put two runners on base and, with two out, their clean-up hitter stepped up to bat. The School for the Deaf pitcher, who was a good friend of Dad's, threw a strike past him, then a ball. The batter then hit one a long way—but foul. Dad ran up to the pitcher and they huddled for a minute. Because they were deaf and always "talked" with a great deal of animation, the umpires didn't watch them closely and the pitcher was able to "load up" the baseball like Big League spitball pitchers did. Dad ran back to his position and the pitcher kicked and pitched.

As Dad described it, the ball dipped just as the batter started to swing. He missed it by a foot. The School for the Deaf team rushed to the bench and the first man up grabbed a bat. They wanted to score before the game was called.

Dad was to be the second batter up that inning. The lead off hitter was a little fellow who could run really fast. The coach signed to him to bunt and he dropped one down the third base line. The Livermore third baseman rushed in and the pitcher came over as the ball trickled down

the chalk mark. When he tells the story, Dad pantomines their movements; they crouch like predatory hawks waiting to grab the ball the
minute it rolls foul. But the ball didn't roll foul and the batter made it
safely all the way to second base.

"Okay, Hank," the coach told Dad. "It's getting dark. You win it for us."

Dad tossed aside one of the two bats he'd been swinging. *I was a
wonderfully good hitter,* he once told me, preferring truth to false mod-
esty. As he strode towards the plate, the Livermore coach came onto the
field. He signalled for a new pitcher, a righthander to replace the
lefthander who'd been throwing against the School for the Deaf. He was a
big kid, the ace of the staff, who not only could throw hard but who also
had a fast-breaking curve ball.

Dad tapped the plate with his bat and scraped the dirt with his spikes
to get a good footing. The Livermore righthander wound up and fired.
Dad swung—and missed, a curve in tight. *I was nervous about that pitch,*
he admitted, demonstrating how he knocked the dirt from his spikes and
stepped back in, crowding the plate just slightly. The righthander fired
again, a fast ball. That was the pitch Dad wanted. He smashed the ball
past the third baseman down the left field line. The runner on second
rounded third and crossed the plate well ahead of the outfielder's throw.
The School for the Deaf had won 3-2 and Dad's teammates rushed out to
hug him and pat him on the back.

"So you were the big hero that day?" I remember asking him.

Instinctively he responded, *"Oh! and many other days too!"* And he
smiled as only he can, so eager and anxious to be believed that none of his
children ever doubted him.

Despite the complaints, Avo himself did a lot to support Dad's
participation in athletic events. Dad's youngest brother Frank, who later
became an excellent athlete himself, remembered that Avo used to take
Dad to Orland and Willows to play softball with a team from the Willows
Portuguese lodge. Though only sixteen, and the "baby" of the team, Dad
was talented enough to play shortstop for the lodge. The team's manager
phoned Avo every spring to extract a promise that "we can have Henry
out there in the infield" and Avo faithfully and, I suspect, proudly took
time off to drive Dad to every practice and every game, even those which
the team played out of town.

In addition, Avo occasionally hosted parties for Dad and some of his
school friends. "It was chaos," Frank remembered. "They all appeared
hyper. There was lots of noise, lots of laughing. Leroy Pate, who was a
C.S.D. athlete like Dad, Kenny Snider, and others would come. They had
a hell of a good time."

Frank, thirteen years younger than Dad, virtually idolized his deaf
older brother. "I thought he was about the greatest athlete in the world,"
he laughed. He also liked Leroy, who like Dad was a good-looking natural

athlete. "I couldn't believe how far they could throw a football. And when they threw a baseball, those old gloves of theirs really popped!

Dad and Kenny Snider, a friend from C.S.D., often took off to go to baseball games in Sacramento or Woodland or to football games at Yuba College, a junior college in Yuba City, some 40 miles southeast of Willows. And they'd go hunting and fishing together.

Each summer during those high school years, Dad worked on the ranch and was a very capable dairyman. Avo's only complaint concerned Dad's love of athletics. "He was always going to some baseball game, or football game. Even after he was married, he couldn't get his mind off of sports." Avo, himself, still liked baseball, but was less of a fan than Dad. And he couldn't understand why sensible beings would want to butt heads and hurt each other on a football field.

Dad had relatively few close friends outside the family. One exception was Max Wampler, a Willows shoe-repairman, and his wife Harriet. The Wamplers, like Father, were deaf. Dad evidently met them one summer after he had begun attending school in Berkeley and Max took a liking to him. Dad, always gregarious, stopped to talk to Max whenever he was in town and the shoe-repairman applauded Dad's athletic exploits, optimism and good looks.

Max Wampler was a tall and good humored man. He and Harriet, a short and caring woman, were quite a bit older than Dad and had five children of their own (all of whom had normal hearing). They understood Dad's strivings and frustrations and could be sympathetic with the problems that his deafness brought him. A warm friendship developed, one which Dad renewed every summer. I think Max became a sort of surrogate father to Dad—someone that he could relate, to both as a parent-type and as a deaf friend.

Dad's brother John told me. "Max was a very devoted friend. He could convince Henry what was the right thing to do. Your Dad regarded him as kind of a Guardian Angel."

"It's too bad," he continued, "that your Dad doesn't have him, or someone like him, through the years. Max would have helped your Dad. Whenever Henry would feel down or get upset or have an argument, he could talk it over with Max. Henry takes a lot of things home with him, like all of us do, things he can't talk to his wife about. If he had someone like Max, a man, he could get them off his chest and Max would understand him."

Except for Max Wampler, Dad's role models lived in totally separate worlds. In many ways, of course, Dad wanted to be like Avo. But he never was able to communicate effectively with his father, and often felt rejected by Avo, particularly when he saw John get favors and authority that Dad thought he had coming as Avo's oldest son. And at the school in Berkeley, the older deaf boys—particularly the athletes that Father

watched when he was in the younger grades—lived in separate, seques-
tered worlds that didn't overlap those outside of the school.

Max Wampler, on the other hand, lived in both worlds. As Dad grew up
to be a friendly, confident teenager, he continued to accept the Wampler's
invitations to visit, to hold conversations, to play cards. Both Wamplers
were fond of whist, a game Dad had learned while in school. These
visits—and card games—eventually led him to seek out the girl who used
to ride with him on the train from Willows to Berkeley and invite her to
form an evening foursome.

That was the first step towards courtship that would lead into marriage.

CHAPTER V

Max Wampler leaned back on the chair in the tiny shoestore and laughed. *What do you think?* he signed to Harriett, who was stirring a pitcher of iced tea over the counter. *Did Henry really score that touchdown or did he fumble the ball in his own end zone?* Dad jumped to his feet, defending the story he had just told, and Max laughed again. *All right, all right, I believe you. I know what kind of a star you were.*

As Harriett served the two men, Max looked out the window. Attracting Dad's attention, he signed *Guess who I saw on the street today?*

Dad shrugged and Max continued *Mildred Carriere. She's a real pretty woman.*

So? Dad was unimpressed. He's known Mom since he first went to school in Berkeley and saw her during the summers every Sunday at Church.

So? Max chided back. *Why don't you take her out sometime? A good-looking guy like you shouldn't have any trouble convincing her.*

Mildred's an old woman! Dad signed to Max. (Mom, then 24, did seem middle-aged to Dad, who had just turned 19.)

Max waved his hand in dismay and glanced at his wife. *They don't make men these days like they did when I was young!* He winked and drew her into the conversation. *Can you imagine me passing up someone like that without even trying to get to know her? So she's a few years older? Do you think that would have stopped me?*

Harriett giggled. Dad frowned. Max knew exactly how to needle him without making him mad. Dad prided himself on his assertiveness and Max had backed him into a corner. *I don't need to worry* he signed to Max. *I'm planning to go back to Oakland and meet some women there.*

Sure! Max raised his eyebrows *and what kind of women are they going to be? As pretty as Mildred? As nice? You go down there and you don't know what you're going to get!*

Again Dad shrugged. *Maybe you're right* he conceded. *And Mildred's okay, I guess. I mean, for somebody older like she is.*

Sure Max agreed. He glanced at Harriett, then snapped his fingers. *I'll bet she plays whist! We could invite her over here! Make a foursome of it!*

Now Dad was pushed into a corner. He couldn't back off without exposing himself to further teasing. He faked a yawn. *Well, if you want to go to that trouble, it's okay with me.* Max wrapped his big hand around Dad's shoulder and, before changing the subject, remarked again *She really is pretty. Very pretty.*

The Wamplers, good to their word, arranged that first "date" of Mom's and Dad's. When I asked Gram about it, she acknowledged that they'd extended the invitation and Mom, quite cheerfully, had accepted it. However, like many things that Mom "accepted," it may have been presented to her as something already arranged, rather than something about which she had an actual choice.

Gram shrugged off her role in that early phase of the matchmaking. For a long time, I was under the impression that Gram and Papa didn't know the Wamplers. "Oh!" I remember Gram telling me, "they were your father's friends. They were friends of the Enoses." But Willows is such a small town, and the Wamplers were such long-time residents there, that I found it odd that the Carrieres hadn't met them, particularly since Max and Harriett were deaf and both had attended the School for the Deaf in Berkeley. But since the Carrieres were farm people, and traveled so exclusively among relatives, I accepted the explanation until Harriett Wampler herself told me that she had known Mom since Mom was a little girl and once had gone to see Gram and Papa because she was concerned about Mom's progress at the Catholic School for the Deaf in Oakland.

As nearly as I can gather, this meeting took place when Mom was nine or ten. Harriett had come across Mom several times in town and discovered that she signed very badly for someone who was supposed to be getting an education. She discussed this matter with her husband, then went to see Papa and Gram.

They were quite surprised to find out that anyone should think that Mom wasn't getting an adequate education. Harriett told me many years later, they were defensive about the Catholic school and dismissed her suggestion that they move Mom to Berkeley. Gram draws herself in and becomes stubborn when she's criticized; perhaps she felt that Harriett Wampler had challenged hers and Papa's good judgement. She told Harriett that she didn't want Mom to leave her friends. And, she added, "After all it is a Catholic school!"

A Catholic school. Remember, Gram and Papa, raised in rural Glenn County with its provincial values, had sent their child to school in a strange city. How did they know who to trust? What kind of a crowd would she get in with if she weren't protected? Gram seemed to feel that the nuns would look out for Mom—even if they didn't teach her anything. And Gram didn't know for sure that the nuns weren't adequate teachers. Both she and Papa detected a lot of improvement in Mom's abilities to take care of herself and communicate. From their standpoint, Mom was doing fine.

But Max and Harriett had correctly assessed Mom's deficiencies. I have no doubts that the nuns tried to be very conscientious, but they were limited by their own shortcomings and taught sign from books, as an auxiliary language; consequently, they often made mistakes.

Unlike Mom, Harriett had been born with hearing. When she was two-and-a-half years old, she contracted rheumatic fever; after a long struggle she recovered, but never was able to hear again. Her parents had moved from Idaho to Magalia, in the foothills east of Chico, when she was very young, then to Los Molinos, a farming community in Tehama County north and east of Willows. She met Max through his sisters. He was eight years older than she, a big, strapping man who was able to support himself even though he was almost totally deaf.

Both Max and Harriett could speak, although Harriett was difficult to understand. Max didn't become totally deaf until he was almost 40 years old. I supposed both Dad and Mom saw them as go-betweens in contact with both the deaf world and the hearing world. Certainly Max acted in the capacity for my father. Harriett remembered that Avo, on a number of occasions, would come to Max and ask him to talk to Dad. In his typically blunt, outspoken manner, Avo would shake his fist, or stamp his foot, "I can't get through to that kid! You make him understand!" and Max, who was older than Avo, would translate Avo's dictums to the determinedly stubborn, and sometimes sulking, boy. Almost invariably Dad would respond, and Max would tell Avo what his son felt. In the process, a true peacemaker, he would tone down Dad's anger and make Avo's demands seem more rational and affectionate than they sometimes were.

"Henry loved Max!" Harriett remembered. Dad trusted the big shoemaker and it was this trust that led him to respect Max's judgments concerning my mother. Max and Harriett did everything that they could to make that first date a success—and, from all accounts, it was. The "old woman" wasn't, Dad discovered, "near half-bad." She was fresh and neat and impeccably dressed, Gram had seen to that, good-natured and just a little bit shy. And Mom, to her surprise, found that "the Enos boy" who she had escorted back and forth to Berkeley on the train years before had become an out-going, assertive, fun-loving—but quite polite—young man.

Max let his guests know that he enjoyed their company very much. Before they left, separately, (neither of them drove and rides had to be arranged to get them back to their respective homes), he suggested another get-together and the suggestion was accepted. That second card party led to a third and then a fourth; by the end of the summer, those visits to the Wamplers' house had become a Saturday night ritual.

In Glenn County, then and now, Sunday dinner was an important event—one that needed to be shared and enjoyed by as many people as possible. In keeping with the times, Papa invited Dad to dinner and Dad, of course, accepted. Gram fixed one of her specialties and Mom baked a dessert. She was, in Gram's words "the best cook! Oh! she made good cakes!" Dad was appropriately impressed and Papa and Gram came away with a new impression of the Enos boy.

"I never would have thought it," Gram referred to her memories of the sniveling youngster who didn't want to get on the train, "but Henry had grown up to be a fine young man."

Just when they decided that Dad was the ideal man for their daughter I don't know. But I do know that they both openly encouraged the relationship. "They kind of pushed you into it, didn't they?" I once teased Dad. *Oh no!* he shook his head *I wanted it!* Max and Harriett continued their intermediary roles, on hand to counsel and advise as well as entertain. And Dad, aware of his dependencies on them and others, walked up to his father and told him *I want to learn to drive a car.*

Athlete that he was, Dad quickly mastered the mechanics of starting, shifting and steering. He learned to depend upon the rear-view and side-view mirrors to compensate for being unable to hear cars behind and beside him, which made him both attentive and more aware of traffic. Also, like most deaf people, by sense of touch he acquired skills that aren't available to most hearing drivers. For instance, he can feel the engine catch when he starts a vehicle, and he can feel a rough or out-of-balance tire or rattling tailpipe. After a few trial runs, Avo shrugged and made his various vehicles—cars, trucks, tractors—available to Dad when he needed one of them.

Avo may not have had any doubts about Dad's abilities behind the wheel, but Gram did. "I didn't know what kind of a driver he was! I used to worry every time Mildred left the house with him!" But she didn't stand in the way of the couples new-found mobility and Dad and Mom stretched their boundaries by going to movies in Willows, taking Sunday drives and going to church together in addition to playing cards with the Wamplers.

Dad was still less than a year out of high school and many of his former athletic teammates lived in the Oakland-Berkeley area. Mom had lost contact with most of her old friends, but still felt an attachment to the school and the Bay Area deaf community. Dad and Mom decided to make an Oakland trip together, Mom to stay with relatives and Dad a friend. *We were just friends then* Dad explained, *nothing had yet been decided upon.* Together they went to the Deaf Club in Oakland, a community-sponsored gathering place that offered a variety of YMCA-type activities.

Dad's face lights up when he describes the visit. A number of his friends are there, plus some people older than him but younger than mother. Most of them are casually dressed and single; some of the women—his face coils distastefully—are smoking cigarettes. They all look up when he enters with Mom. She is, he shows you, fresh and clean and dressed very nicely. For a moment, no one says anything—they just stare. Then one of his friends comes up to be introduced. Dad boasts. *He is jealous that I have such a good-looking woman with me.*

And Dad admits *I was proud. I kind of showed your Mom off. It made me realize how fortunate I was to have met someone like her in Glenn County.*

But Dad wasn't ready to commit himself—not yet. Despite the open and approving reception that he received each time he came to the Carrieres' house, "Oh!" Gram told me, "I loved Henry from the time he and Mildred first dated!" Dad insisted that he needed to look the field over a little longer. He arranged another Oakland trip—but this time he went alone, admittedly *to check out the women down there.* He and his friends went to ball games and to some of the old school hang-outs and they culled their respective address books for the names of girls they knew or wanted to meet.

He stayed almost three weeks. But the women down there didn't look as good as they had before. They neither were as pretty, nor as friendly, nor as comfortable to be with as he'd imagined they might be. He decided to return to Willows and *take a look at Mildred again.*

The first date after he returned started a bit coldly. Mom wanted to know where he had been—and what he had been doing. Dad tried to pass the visit off as *a chance to see old friends, and play some baseball,* but Mom saw through the subterfuge. She wanted to know if he had *"seen any women down there"* and Dad shrugged and admitted *just a few.*

Well, then, maybe you don't want to go out with me?

Oh no! I want to go out with you even more now!

I don't think so.

Yes! I really do!

Mom tried to look less than interested. *Why?* she wanted to know.

"And then what happened?" I broke in.

Oh! Dad grinned *I kissed her a lot!*

Either Dad had told Avo why he was making the trip to Oakland, or Avo and Grandma Enos had guessed what had motivated it, for Grandma cornered Dad one evening soon after his return. She asked him a few questions about Oakland, then, in her firm, quiet way, suggested, *"Why don't you just take Mildred out for a while? Not worry about anybody else? You both go to the same Catholic Church. You go running around, you don't know what you're going to find. You never know what those women down there in Oakland are like."*

Yes, Dad told me, *I listened to her. But already I had decided the same thing. So I told my mother, yes I am going to take care of that.*

He was good to his word. Avo had given him a gray pick-up, a real clunker, but it ran well and Dad was highly visible around Willows, one hand on the steering wheel and the other around his sweetheart. The young couple's circle of supporters widened; where it had just included family, and close friends like the Wamplers, it now encompassed most of the Willows area. Even relative strangers took pride in "their deaf couple" and people like Max, who knew them, extolled their virtues at great length.

The Carrieres invited Dad over often, and the Enoses had Mom come to dinner at their house as well. Dad expressed an interest in Papa's projects, particularly the new machinery that he was developing; to Mom's dismay, the two of them sometimes spent hours together in Papa's shop. But Dad never really neglected his "girl." He took her to the movies in Willows which, despite being deaf, they both enjoyed, Dad preferring the action features which were easy to follow, Mom the comedies and romances. Try turning off the sound on your television set sometime, and follow the plot of a situation comedy or full-length movie. You might be surprised how much you understand, especially the subtleties conveyed by the actors' and actresses' movements and expressions. The eyes have to do the work that the ears can't do, and the results can be rewarding. Many deaf people invent a plot to fill in the places that they can't understand. These sometimes prove to be both amusing and psychologically revealing.

This rush of going places and doing things, of having a "boy friend" who liked her and kissed her and made a big fuss over her, caused Mom to blossom. Her quiet, boring, lonesome life suddenly had been transformed into something quite exciting. Remember, she had been living in Papa's and Gram's house by the levee for nearly seven years since leaving the School for the Deaf in Berkeley. Neither she nor Gram talk much about those years—probably there isn't a great deal to say about them. Mom's brothers were developing into good-natured, but conscientious, teenagers; Papa was expanding his ranch and presiding over the meetings and projects of the fledgling water district. He continued to work from dawn to dusk six days a week, and to relax, go to church and exchange convivial dinners with his relatives on Sundays.

While he was thus engaged, Gram had continued to play both mother and nursemaid to her deaf daughter. She was a behind-the-scenes force in Mom's romance with my father. Gram sewed clothes and checked Mom's appearance and watched the clock to make sure that Mom was ready when Dad swung by to pick her up. This was important, since Mom often forgot about clocks completely and my father tended to be brash and somewhat impatient, not the type to humbly sit for hours while his sweetheart ironed her clothes or curled her hair.

The privacy of traveling by car enabled Mother to relax and talk in sign without the embarrassment she sometimes felt in public. She didn't have to worry about somebody watching her and thinking she was unusual, or strange, or a misfit. And Father, being so out-going, and affable, and eager to please, was good for her. Mom wasn't anti-social, but she certainly did not push her way into conversations with strangers. I think it's possible that by taking such good care of Mom, by making her feel so special and so well-loved, Gram may have hindered her from adapting in the more rough-and-tumble way that Father did. Both at home, and at the school in Berkeley, Mother had been encapsuled in a small, secure world and she felt quite uncomfortable when she left it.

Dad refused to submerge himself in that world. He had begun to see himself as heir to his father's worldly position—a well-to-do-mid-Valley dairyman who was respected by his peers and who was a cornerstone of Saint Monica's Catholic Church in Willows. He had no desire to hide from people, or to cover his deafness by feigning that he could hear and understand those things that escaped him. Instead he would push to make himself understood, and to understand others. He literally could invent a deaf language—a language of gestures—that the non-deaf could use. That failing, he would yank pad and pencil from his pocket and write what he was trying to say. He was, as they say, going to get full measure for all his goods.

Even so, there were problems that the young lovers found that they had to face. One was the age difference that separated them. Mom, in particular, felt very self-conscious about this. Gram told me that she once found the two of them poring over the Vital Statistics column in the local newspaper, a flutter of excitement greeting the rare discovery of a marriage license issued to a couple whose differences in ages corresponded to theirs. Always the diplomat, unobtrusive but persistent, Gram pointed out that Mom's Aunt Anna was several years older than her Uncle Pete and "—they've had a very wonderful marriage."

Also, there were doubts that a deaf couple could succeed or even survive as homemakers, wage earners, potential parents. Papa and Gram in particular discussed this when Mom's and Dad's relationship reached the serious stage. Had they not owned their own land, and instead been townspeople confined by a 40-hour-a-week job in a factory or office, they might have been more hesitant about the prospects of their daughter marrying someone who might have difficulty supporting her. But the Carrieres, though by no means rich, had resources to offer a son-in-law like Dad, whom they liked very much and who Papa appraised as a good worker. And the Enoses, on their side, were prepared to back Dad as well.

The young couple "officially" set their engagement for September 8, Mom's birthday. A few weeks earlier, Avo had taken Dad to Willows and they'd selected an engagement ring. Impishly, after he had wrapped the gift, Dad collected a series of boxes that would fit one within the other and wrapped each of them. No occasion ever became so serious that one couldn't have a little fun with it, he thought.

Engagement parties were held at both the Carrieres' house and the Enoses'. And though both families had openly approved the match for a long time, it was an emotional occasion for all concerned. Gram vividly remembers the trip to the Enos farm. She and Mom spent hours getting ready. Mom wore red—Dad's favorite color. "She was tense and excited—but brimming with happiness," Gram remembered. "She sat in the front seat between me and Papa. As we got close to Willows, she reached towards each of us and gave our hands a gentle squeeze. Then she signed to me, and to Papa, 'I love you.'

"I grabbed her and gave her a big hug. My eyes were filled with tears as I signed 'I love you' to her and glanced to Papa. He was sitting stiff and erect behind the wheel, tears streaming down his cheeks. It was a truly happy moment for all three of us."

Meanwhile, Dad was experiencing the anxiety and confusion common to young men on their wedding day. Grandma Enos described him as "all aflutter. He couldn't get the knot in his necktie to look the way he wanted and his hands were shaking so bad he couldn't tie his shoes. I had to come to his rescue!" Not sure whether she wanted to laugh or cry, she got Father to sit on the edge of the bed while she tied his shoes.

She was straightening his tie, nodding and assuring him that he looked all right, when Avo came in. He gestured to Father that he would tie the necktie. "There we were, in the middle of the room, fretting over the tie, and Henry lifted his head and blinked," Grandma Enos remembered. "He put his arms around us to hug us and then he started to cry. We hugged him and patted his back—whether we were laughing or crying, I don't know which—then pulled away to sign to him to hurry, the Carrieres will be here soon. Henry wiped his eyes and was still straightening and smoothing his necktie when we left the room."

When she saw Gram and Papa arrive with the bride-to-be, Grandma Enos rushed to her son's bedroom, signalled *Come, come!* and pointed in the direction of the door. Despite his excitement, Dad managed to contain his emotions and play the host. He greeted the Carrieres with a hug and Mildred with a kiss on the cheek. "They were so polite," Gram remembered, "and they both were radiant. The energy and happiness pouring through them affected us all."

Avo invited his guests into the livingroom and brought each of them a drink. Avo and Papa talked about farming and Gram joined Grandma Enos in the kitchen. Father and Mother sat next to each other holding hands. They didn't need spoken words to communicate to each other and neither set of parents doubted that the young couple was deeply in love.

The formal announcement of the engagement came at dinner. When both families were seated, Avo circled the table and poured champagne for everyone. Then, from the head of the table, he proposed a toast. "I would like to make an announcement. Henry and Mildred are going to be married."

Gram remembered the fiances' nervous and excited smiles. She caught their attention and signed *Do you want to get married?* Instinctively they responded *Yes!* "They were so excited they hardly could keep themselves in their chairs," Gram laughed. "Their enthusiasm was contagious. We drank to their happiness. All of us were filled with enthusiasm and animation. Suddenly Henry jumped up and bolted out of the room. He returned a minute later with the package that he'd wrapped for Mildred. Everyone laughed as box after box came out, each one smaller than its predecessor, until Mildred finally got down to the ring."

She gasped—as most young brides do—and passed the ring around so that everybody could see it. Only her little brother Herb, then 11, refused to look at it. "He wanted nothing to do with such silly, mushy stuff," Gram laughed.

Dad slipped the ring on Mom's finger—or tried to. As well-coordinated as Dad was, the super athlete who could dribble a basketball behind his back while racing full-speed down the court or turn a double-play so quickly that you hardly knew he had the ball, he couldn't get the ring to fit. The harder he tried, the more nervous he got; those watching broke into bursts of sympathetic laughter. Finally, with Mom's help, he succeeded and heaved a big sigh.

Papa signalled to Dad to kiss Mom, but Dad didn't pick up the cue. He stood there sighing and grinning and Mom grinned—she was so happy she had tears in her eyes. Again Papa gestured to Dad *Kiss her! you should kiss her now!* Avo laughed—so did Grandma Enos. Dad just stood there beaming, still so caught up in his own feelings that he didn't perceive what they were trying to get him to do.

Finally, Gram beside him laughing and shaking her head, Papa caught Dad's attention. For an instant he looked startled, as though asked to do something he never should do in public, then he smiled and nodded and took his bride-to-be in his arms. This time he kissed her on the lips, not the cheek. Herb covered his face with his hands and groaned, but Mom and Dad held onto each other until Avo gestured to his son to sit down. By this time, Grandma Enos was urging everyone, "Come on. Dinner's getting cold. Let's eat." But as far as the young lovers were concerned, the meal hardly existed. As in the song, they only had eyes for each other. While the others filled their plates, they held hands and smiled at each other.

That afternoon at the Enoses' house marked the end of their difficult growing up years. Despite their handicaps, they had managed to achieve those things considered "normal" by most young people their age; they'd gone to school, fallen in love and were going to be married. I'm sure they imagined that they were embarking on a very joyful and exciting adventure together and, in fact, they were. At the same time, I wonder if they had any idea how dependent upon their parents each of them, in different ways, had been until that moment? Did they have any concept of what working and rearing children as deaf parents in a totally non-deaf world would be like? Did they wonder—or worry—about each other's abilities or deficiencies?

Probably, like most of us when we fall in love, they were so enthused and happy that they viewed the future through rose-colored lenses. Everything seems so simple when you have someone to share things with—of course it will go on forever! Even if they could have seen a preview of all of the difficulties that lay ahead of them, would that have dissuaded them?

I hope not. Their deafness had brought them together and was an integral part of their feelings for each other. Certainly their lives and futures in this isolated farming country took on new meaning as their friendship deepened into love. Gram insists that God marked them for this special union when He took away their hearing. I wouldn't argue with that at all.

The wedding was one of the biggest social events of the year. Hundreds of people—many of them only slight acquaintances of the Enos and Carriere families—came to see the deaf couple get married in St. Monica's parish church in Willows. Father Rielley from the Berkeley School for the Deaf appeared with the parish's Father McGoldrick to translate the rites into sign for Dad and Mom.

The church was decked with flowers. Mom was radiant in a white wedding dress purchased for the occasion. Gram made matching blue dresses for the three bridesmaids and herself. Remember, she had described how special this wedding would be when she persuaded my mother to return to Willows to stay, even though my father was not, at that time, in the picture as a suitor.

Dad and his brother John, who was his best man, stood stiff and formal in black tuxedoes. Papa, also in a tuxedo, gave the bride away. Father Rielley interpreted each word for Mom and Dad and they made their replies in sign, which Father Rielley, in turn, relayed to the congregation, which included a number of Mom's and Dad's deaf friends from the Berkeley school.

If you've never seen a ceremony for the deaf relayed in sign, you should seek out the opportunity just for the aesthetic beauty transmitted by such an occasion. Father Rielley's interpretation of the sermon, and the rites, contained all the elements of classical ballet. He signed fluidly, with a sense of rhythm and depth that enhanced the meanings of the words for all those in attendance. Many people afterwards told him, and told Gram and Papa and the Enoses, that they had followed his interpretations as avidly as the deaf guests did. "It was beautiful! Absolutely beautiful! I really felt—really deeply—everything that was going on!" one long-time Willows resident, a friend of Papa's and Gram's, enthused during the reception.

The wedding, and the festivities that followed it in the old parish hall, proceeded just exactly as Gram had promised my mother that they would. In many ways, it typified her treatment of Mom, for Gram never lost awareness of Mom's deafness and continually compensated for it. I think she perceived deafness as a minus, a negative, and was determined to heap as much plusses around her daughter as she possibly could. Certainly that's what she did on this occasion.

The reception included a sit-down dinner for more than 300 guests "—turkey and ham and all the trimmings," my uncle remembered. The Portuguese love celebrations, particularly those which bring families together; Mom's and Dad's wedding surpassed most of those within memory. An orchestra was hired and beer and champagne flowed. The beer—big, icy kegs of it—was Avo's idea, even though it was unusual to serve it at a wedding. Perhaps he anticipated that with such a large gathering, crossing so many ethnic lines, that it would be appreciated.

Both sets of parents still describe the "obvious happiness" on the young couple's faces as they swung around the dancefloor on their solo dance. With a crowd around them, they cut into the tiered wedding cake and shoved the first pieces into each other's mouths. Then, as the dancing continued, they changed into their going-away outfits and reemerged for a last flurry of kisses and congratulations, then ran out of the hall under a fusillade of rice.

Then as now, strings of tin cans were tied to the back bumper of the "getaway car." At Dad's and Mom's wedding, everything was done to excess, so it's not surprising that the brothers and cousins out-did themselves. According to Papa, they used 10-gallon containers that made so much racket they could be heard all the way across town, especially when the car picked up speed.

But Dad didn't hear them. Flushed and happy, one hand on the steering wheel and the other around his bride's shoulder, he swung out of Willows, setting hackles on edge and causing dogs to howl. Probably more than one motorist honked, but of course Dad couldn't hear them either. Nor could he hear the Highway Patrolman's siren.

Dad loves to relate the story to anyone who'll watch him. Yes, he nods, he did see the flashing lights and with his hands he shows you how they spin and blink and how he pulled over to the right to let the police car pass. His face expresses his surprise when the car stops behind him. The patrolman's face, he shows you, is stern and angry. He shows you how the officer jabs his finger, thinking that, he gestures, because I cannot talk that I am drunk. Mother is startled and worried. The patrolman's flashlight, Dad squints, is shining directly into my eyes. Finally, Dad produces his license—his marriage license!—to prove that he and Mom have just been married and are heading out on their honeymoon.

Dad's face relaxes as he shows you the patrolman's laugh. He shows you how the officer beckons him out of the car and points to the string of battered cans. He imitates the patrolman motioning him to untie them, then he shows you how he looks down at his neatly tailored, new traveling clothes.

His face breaks into a grin. He gestures to the officer, *'See how nicely I am dressed. Why don't you do it for me so I don't get myself all dirty?'* His eyes sparkle as he nods and shows you that the patrolman does, indeed, remove the cans from the car for him.

That he can detach himself from situations like this and laugh at himself and what he does, even on his wedding night, always has helped Dad to function in the hearing world. He is, in such situations, as naive as he is good-hearted. I think the patrolman who stopped him that night must have realized that. And I hope in telling the story himself he has exaggerated it a little bit.

Dad always appreciates being the star.

CHAPTER VI

The infield is coated with dust and the outfield, between the basepaths and an unpainted wooden fence, is uneven, its grass brownish-green and worn bald where the outfielders stand. The teams playing softball are wearing bright-colored uniforms, except for the third baseman, apparently a fill-in from some other team, for he has only a gray sweatshirt and rumpled cap bearing the logo of a now defunct professional franchise. Coming to bat is my father, young, robust, recently married. The coach along the first base line claps his hands. Dad rubs dirt between his palms and takes a strong practice swing. Before he steps into the batter's box, he looks over his shoulder at his pretty young wife.

The first pitch is high, but the second breaks across the strike zone. Dad smashes it past the third baseman and turns first, heading for second. The outfielder charges the ball, drops it, scrambles for it as it rolls a few feet away. As he rounds second, Dad sees him fumbling it and takes off for third. Mom leaps to her feet, clapping, as the outfielder finally recovers the ball and fires a good throw into third. Dad hits the dirt, hooking away from the base as he kicks up dust with his slide.

The umpire, out of position and late to anticipate the play, hesitates, then flings his right thumb upward. "Out!" he shouts, "You're out!"

Dad whirls. He runs towards him, vigorously shaking his head. *The throw was late! He missed me! He didn't tag me! He didn't have hold of the ball!* But he can't say those words and he has to use his hands. Dramatically he shows the third baseman bobbling the ball, swiping at an imaginary runner. His hands shoot outward in a safe gesture. The umpire shakes his head and Dad becomes even more livid. Again he gestures *Safe! Safe!*

Dad's teammates rush out to get between him and the umpire. *"Hey, Henry, we're five runs ahead!" "C'mon, it's not a league game!" "Hey, play ball, let's just have fun!"* They tried to quiet him down. He turns to them, still gesturing that he beat the throw, or the third baseman dropped it. They nod, agree, and he goes back to the bench, still angry.

So the umpire was wrong—the rest of the team doesn't really care. "Hey, he's not getting paid, let's not get too rough on him," they say to each other. But to Dad the call at third was more than just an arbitrary decision in a sandlot softball game. It was frustration itself. It was someone not hearing what he wanted to say. It was that impenetrable wall that he found facing him and it ignited his deepest feelings.

The knowledge is there, the will power is there, but the vehicle for expressing confused and complicated sentiments often failed my father—

as it fails deaf people so often. He knew that he was safe because he felt his foot hit the bag before he felt the tag. But he couldn't express it, not in words—not in those words. Even on the bench, talking in animated sign language to two of his teammates, he couldn't force that knowledge, that complex set of intuitions and awareness, into conversational language. He couldn't lean back, shift a wad of tobacco or gum from one cheek to the other, spit and say, "That's the third call that turkey's missed already today," and forget the incident. Dad just couldn't do it.

Events like that didn't occur only on the softball field. Many times during Dad's life he was confronted with situations that couldn't be resolved in the present, using the language of the deaf. His hands would flash the words he knew—if they were inadequate he would get excited, or angry, or violent. Once, after a dispute in one of Avo's alfalfa fields, he took after his brother John with a pitchfork. On another occasion he got red-faced and angry with Avo because he knew a crop wasn't ready to be cut and Avo had told him to cut it. But he couldn't explain what he could see and feel with his fingers. Avo thought he was just being stubborn or trying to get out of doing the work. The language wasn't there for Dad to communicate all that he knew.

Soon after Dad and Mom returned from their honeymoon and moved in with Mom's parents "—until something can be arranged of your own—" Dad had to make a decision that would substantially change the way he would live the rest of his life. Papa had offered him a permanent job on the Carriere ranch, and Dad, for all intents and purposes, had accepted it. But how was the offer made? Did Papa, in sign, say *You can work here for as long as you like?* Did Papa mean forever? Or did Dad understand him to say *as long as I like—until I find something else?* Miscommunications like that occur all the time among the deaf.

Then Avo offered Dad a partnership of sorts—the business would be his and his brothers to inherit when he retired or died. Both his offer and the one from Papa included a housing arrangement: Papa intended to build on a lot he'd purchased in Willows and Avo had acquired some land near Bayliss, which contained a newly constructed house. Dad was working for Papa. He was, the Carrieres insisted "a good worker, a very conscientious worker." He had leaped into his place on Papa's ranch with enthusiam and vigor. Robust and athletic and anxious to please his employer-father-in-law, Dad spent ten to twelve to fourteen hours a day on Papa's tractors. "They were old machines, but good ones, and your Dad loved to drive them," Papa remembered.

And he drove them well. Herb contended, "He was the straightest driver in the field. You never saw any straighter furrows." Dad himself will describe them to anyone who'll listen, lifting one arm and sighting along it to show that not a waver or ripple appears anywhere along it as far as the eye can see.

As temperatures soared past 100, to 110, and above, Dad got tanner but, according to Papa and Gram "—his enthusiasm for hard work didn't wane a bit." He irrigated, cultivated, repaired ditch banks and barns, overhauled equipment and hauled pick-up loads of fertilizer to the fields and brush to the dump. The busy routine didn't force him to abandon his first love, however. On weekends and some evenings he'd tuck a baseball glove in his pocket and go off somewhere to play.

Despite his frustrations and difficulties with communication, Dad forged a feeling of being equal, both on the ranch and on the ball field. He didn't try to hide his deafness and he often laughed about the inconveniences it caused him. Herb remembered that he was always burning himself in the shop. "He couldn't hear us say that this piece of metal or that piece of metal was hot. He was always grabbing something that somebody had just heated up. We were always kidding him about that."

Dad, always expressive and an excellent mimic, would shake his hand, blow on it, make *wow! wow! wow!* sounds that the others would imitate and they'd all wind up laughing together. Papa decided to purchase a lot in Willows and build a house on it that Mom and Dad could live in. Dad was working for Papa and was receiving wages and he was also, of course, getting room and board. He had not, however, completely broken ties with Avo. Apparently, sometime during that summer, or several times during the course of the summer, Avo talked to him concerning the Enos dairy business. I don't know how thoroughly Dad understood the offer, or how carefully Avo explained it. Nor do I know how long Dad mulled it over, balancing one opportunity against the other. Finally, at any rate, he chose to go with Avo.

Although accepted into the Carriere family, Dad's position with Papa basically was that of a hired man. John Enos, Dad's younger brother, was in high school at the time, but remembered some mention of friction between Avo and the Carrieres. "I have in mind that the Carrieres may have asked Mom and Dad to put up money for part of the house, or the lot—I'm not sure what it was. I guess, instead Avo bought the property near Bayliss."

Avo, unlike Papa, was impulsive. The land near Bayliss was for sale—Avo liked the looks of it and probably got a good price on it. He may simply have decided to purchase it rather than go in with the Carrieres on the property in town. Quite possibly he didn't bother to tell them what he was doing. And I doubt that Dad knew much about either transaction, either before it happened or afterwards.

The details of that misunderstanding probably are less significant than the outcome. The Carrieres quietly withdrew their financial support and Dad became dependent upon Avo for everything from cash to cars to houses to clothes. "Dependent" is both an accurate and a loaded word; as children, we kids were keenly aware that we had to go to, or through, Avo and Uncle John for the things we needed and we often felt like little Cinderella's with no resources of our own. On the other hand, Dad was put on equal footing with John in the partnership, and John was scrupulously honest about the way he ran the ranch.

I don't want to give the impression that Gram and Papa crawled away to sulk or pout. They accepted Dad's decision. Mom still was their only child and they were determined to support her emotionally, if not financially. I've often wondered what effect Dad's and Mom's deafness had on the situation. Conceivably the same chain of circumstances could- and would-have occurred if Mom and Dad had been hearing persons. Such struggles for power among children and inlaws occur all the time in farming families. But other sons, or sons-in-laws, might have been able to sit down and talk the situation out, give vent to the confused feelings pulling them first this way, then that way.

I can picture my dad (I know him so well!) sitting at the diningroom table in the Carrieres' house telling Papa and Gram about the dairy, about the work he'd do there. I can see him describing the land, the little house, the tractors. . . . then I discern Papa asking *Why?* and Dad repeating the descriptions—the farm, the dairy, the tractors, the equipment. But *why?* and Dad can sign *my father* even describe Avo's looks, his moods. But *why?* and a gap opens, a ravine that's so tremendously difficult to cross.

It is what I want to do! Dad is an athlete, a dynamic person; the words in sign come across too strong. The vigor of his outburst is not anger, it's a groping for expression. Sometimes people recoil from that vigor, their feelings hurt. Is that what happened with Papa?

Then I see Avo. He is signing, simply *You come to work for me. I am your father. You are my son. The dairy will be yours someday—yours and John's and Frankie's.*

"Okay, Dad. Just what am I going to be doing? How much will I get paid? How often? Well, that's not quite enough. Okay, whose name will the deed for the house be in? What about my playing basketball? I'll want a day-and-a-half each week off. What about a car? You buyin' it, or do I have to provide my own? What about. . . ?

That's what John might say, or Herb or Frank or my husband Clifford. But Dad . . . somehow he wouldn't. Concepts like that are developed from hearing and participating in many conversations—conversations about ideas. Dad has the ideas but didn't grow up expressing them, developing them, refining them. In many ways, being deaf is like being a foreigner in a strange land. You learn the names for things—tomatoes, tractors, babies, cake—but not the philosophy; that culture's particular ideas are hard—almost impossible—to grasp in words that you can use and command.

So the explanations, the softer words, the words that knit and heal, weren't spoken. I know that at gut-level Dad's patrimony tugged at him. He had been born on Avo's ranch, grown up there— it was home and he was Avo's oldest son. Someday it would be his to inherit—his portion of it, at any rate. Certainly his decision conformed to the values that he grew to know. Besides that, the house that Avo was providing was only a year old and was more than adequate for Dad's fledgling family. Avo's dairy business was prospering and Avo had continued to add to both his dairy and his land holdings. Both on the surface and psychologically Dad's choice seemed, at the time, to have been a logical and satisfying one.

Avo grew a large amount of the alfalfa that he fed to his herds and Dad spent most of the first spring and summer on a tractor, ploughing, discing, and planting. Avo himself did the work of at least two men and he expected his sons to follow the example that he set. He was a stern taskmaster who knew what he wanted done; he insisted that his directions be followed to the letter. Dad's younger brother John, though still in high school, already was working full-time for Avo; occasionally Avo would give John some directives to pass on to Dad. This upset Dad on more than one occasion. He didn't like taking "orders" from his younger brother and John, as he later told me "—didn't have any choice. Avo would come down on me if I didn't do what he told me to do." Avo often became frustrated with Sign Language because he couldn't convey his exact thoughts or express himself completely; therefore, he allowed the communication to develop between John and Dad.

Dad and Uncle John were five years apart in age. As boys they'd often played together but "—Henry always was so much bigger than me. And strong!" Because Dad had spent most of his schoolboy years away from home, John virtually grew up as an only child, then as the older of two sons. The youngest of Avo's children, my uncle Frank, was born in 1939, when John was seven years old and Dad was twelve.

A rivalry gradually developed between the two brothers. Dad, I'm sure felt it most keenly. Perhaps because John could hear and talk and consequently got to live at home and didn't have to go away to school, Dad subconsciously thought of him as "privileged," I don't know. At any rate, John continually regarded his bigger, tougher brother with a mixture of fear and respect.

"We used to play a lot of baseball," he told me. "We'd play teams— Ernie, our cousin, and I against Henry and Frankie and Carol Ann, another cousin. Whenever there was a close play that went against your Dad—a tag at the plate or something like that—he'd get mad and chase us around and scream."

On one occasion, John and Dad were playing games near the barn. A misunderstanding arose and John took off running to tell Avo what had happened. Dad started after him with a handful of rocks.

"He had such a good aim," John laughed, "that I ducked behind an old apricot tree—the last rock he'd thrown had come pretty close. There was just a tiny gap between the tree's two main limbs and I'll be damned if the next rock your Dad threw didn't come right through that gap and hit me on the head!

"I went down like I'd been shot. I remember your Dad picking me up to see if I was all right. From the look on his face, I could tell that he thought he'd killed me!"

On another occasion, John cut through a gate to get away from Dad. He glanced back to see how close his pursuer was and ran into a nail protruding from the gatepost. It punctured the flesh near his temple and he flopped backwards, blood pouring across his face. Dad started for Avo, who ran up, grabbed John and rushed him to the doctor.

I asked John about Avo's reaction to the incident, expecting him to say that Avo had given Dad a good whipping. But John replied, "The first thing Avo did was take care of that damned nail. It had no business sticking through that gatepost anyway!"

But there was closeness as well as rivalry in the two brothers' relationship. John was the first in the Enos family to learn sign well enough to communicate efficiently with Dad. Unlike Mom, who early during her schooling had learned sign from nuns who couldn't do it well, Dad became reasonably adept at it at an earlier age. He brought his books and sets of flash cards home each summer and tried to teach John how to form the words.

"But signing for me always was very difficult," John admitted. "I couldn't twist my hands around the way they should go. Your Dad would make fun of my fumbling efforts and I'd want to quit and give it up. Finally, when I was a little older—about when your Dad was in high school—I caught on to what it was all about. It became meaningful to me to want to talk to your Dad. I managed to learn quite a lot.

"This ability with sign, combined with Avo's more limited facility with the language, later put John in an intermediary position between Dad and Avo. As Avo began to pull away from the daily running of the dairy business, he naturally relied on John to convey information or directions to Dad and Dad often felt slighted and sometimes got angry.

While John looked upon Dad as a rival to be treated with a mixture of caution and respect, youngest brother Frankie regarded Dad with unequivocal awe. Dad was a teenaged football, basketball and baseball star when Frank first became aware of him. In the baseball games the family played in a field beside Avo's orchard, Frank—as the youngest—always got to be on Dad's side.

"He had a terrific influence on my life, particularly when it came to sports," Frank, who went on to play halfback for Chico State University and become their all-time rushing leader, remembered. "When he was home we had a great time. I remember playing ball in the rain and mud—probably it was during one Christmas vacation. We'd get so muddy you couldn't see anything but the whites of our eyes. We loved it!"

In those days, Dad was a rabid University of California Bears and St. Mary's University Gaels fan. One day in the early '50's, when television was just coming into the Valley, Dad took Frank to Willows. The Bears game was on TV and one of the bars in downtown Willows had a set. Dad took Frank inside to watch the game. "I guess we saw three or four plays, then somebody in the bar decided I shouldn't be in there and we left," Frank laughed. "But just going there with him was a big deal for me."

Fortunately, during those first years that he worked for Avo, Dad's interests weren't confined to the fields. For the first time in his life, he had a house of his own and he felt good about it—proud. The house, and the fact that he and Mom soon were going to be parents, excited him. On Saturdays, when he went into town, or Sundays at church and at family gatherings afterwards, he compared himself to other men that he saw and knew and found that he equalled them, materially and personally.

He and Mom still visited the Wamplers and Dad continued to play softball during the summer. One fall an old schoolmate from the School for the Deaf recruited Dad for an all-deaf basketball team called the Sacramento Silence. They played most of their home games in Woodland, a seventy-five mile drive from Willows; Avo went through the roof more than once because Dad left work early to make the team's games but Dad stubbornly persisted in going. He loved sports too much to drop them completely. And, as Frank noted, "Sports on weekends were something he could look forward to. His outlook was good. He didn't sit around and stew about things."

One Sunday afternoon Mom and Dad came through the front door. "They had smiles on their faces a mile wide," Gram recalled. Mom ran up to Gram and hugged and kissed her. Then, in sign, she asked *Will you please come into the bedroom?*

Gram could tell that Mom was excited but she wasn't sure just what was going on. Mom pushed the bedroom door closed behind them and began to describe how she was feeling. She signed *I haven't menstrated in two months and my chest is getting full and tight!*

Gram gasped *You're going to have a baby!* she signed.

I know! Mom gestured and clapped her hands. They hugged each other, then hurried into the livingroom where Dad was waiting. Dad and Mom turned to Papa and told him what they thought was happening. Papa jumped to his feet and threw his arms around both of them. Tears began to roll down his face.

You'd better not tell anyone until we're absolutely sure Gram suggested. Dad and Mom glanced at each other, grinned and nodded agreement. For at least a few weeks longer, the secret would remain within the family.

Gram, of course, was excited—and, she admitted later, afraid. "I couldn't help but worry that the baby was going to be deaf. I don't know how much Mildred and your Dad thought about it—maybe it didn't affect them in the same way that it did me. I prayed a great deal, I know that!"

Mom, quite properly, was enthused. Dad already was counting the touchdowns that his first-born son would score. As preparations for the great event grew more detailed, Gram fretted not only about the baby but about how well her daughter would be able to take care of a child. A whole new range of questions and preoccupations thrust their way into the picture. How would Mildred know when her baby was crying? How would she call for help in case of an emergency? How much help would Henry be in raising the child?

Mom spent a good deal of time in her new little two-bedroom house. She never had learned to drive a car, so was restricted to the immediate area except when Dad was home. Gram visited her almost daily. "Oh yes," Gram remembered, "we were very concerned, you know, about the baby. Mildred's doctor said he had no reason to believe that the child wouldn't have normal hearing but, you see, there was no way that we could be certain about it. We just had to wait—and pray."

It was Gram's intention that Mom keep in the best of health while she was pregnant. She arranged frequent visits to the doctor, helped Mom with the shopping and even cleaned house for her on occasion. Those visits set a pattern that continued for nearly twenty-five years. My two older sisters, Donna and Peggy, and I considered Gram as a second mother. Whenever there was a problem we called her—or whenever we just wanted someone to talk to. In the early years, especially, she was visibly so supportive, so intent on making sure we did everything just the way it should be done. She was the one we turned to in case of an emergency, whether it was an overdue book report or a rival cheerleader's snotty comments about us. I don't know what we would have done without her.

Thus it was Gram, not Mom, who stocked in diapers, quilts, pads, crib liners—all those little things that a mother needed. She made telephone calls, wrote notes, had Mom's prescriptions filled. And, like any grandmother, she worried and waited for the "precious arrival," concerned about possible complications and the health and normalcy of her first grandchild.

From the seventh month on, Mom knew that her baby would be just fine. How did she know? Her face glows when she answers the question. *An Angel came and tapped me on the toes!* she insists. Her fingers describe the beautiful visitor whose radiance filled the room with a soft white light. *I woke up and she was standing by the foot of the bed . . .* Mom's fingers created the picture. *She was about four feet tall, plump, with a face that was so smooth and perfectly formed that I couldn't believe*

*that she was real. I blinked and rubbed my eyes—I thought she might go
away, vanish into thin air—but she shook her head to assure me that she
was there and she smiled and told me, in sign, that I was going to have a
perfect baby. . . .*

It's a beautiful story, one that I've watched my mother tell many times.
I believe that it's true. She puts a great deal of faith in it. But once, when
I was retelling it in front of my oldest sister Donna, I was startled to find
her scoffing. "Oh, come on, surely you don't believe that? Mom's been
repeating it for years. I don't think it happened—I think she dreamed it."

"Well," I stuck to my guns, "I want to believe it." But I was aware,
seeing Donna's smile, that I was being as stubborn and romantic as my
Grandmother Carriere. Not everyone, I know, can sustain that kind of
unskeptical, unquestioning belief.

If Mom told Dad about her vision or dream, whichever it was, she didn't
insist that her first-born was going to be a girl. Dad wanted a son. In his
mind's eye, he already could see him seated on his lap on the tractor, or
lifting a baseball bat to slap a fast ball down the line into the left field
corner. Among relatives on both sides of the family, he talked about the
new arrival, using the sign for "boy." He even asked both Gram and
Grandma Enos if they thought the little fellow would look like his father.

Mom stayed with Gram for the last few weeks of her pregnancy. When
she went into labor, Gram rushed her to the hospital. Dad was notified
and drove to town as quickly as he could. *Is it a boy? Is it a boy?* he wanted
to know. Finally the waiting room door opened and a white-clad nurse
stepped into the room.

"Mister Enos?"

Dad jumped up, signing to Gram. The nurse smiled. "It's a girl," she
announced. "Eight pounds and three ounces. Mother and baby both are
doing fine." Dad, of course, reacted with great joy because his first child
born was a healthy and beautiful child.

My oldest sister Donna Marie Enos, the first grandchild on either side
of the family, was bright-eyed and healthy. Initial worries that she might
have inherited Dad's and Mom's deafness gradually were dispelled. Her
doctor couldn't detect any hearing problems and she responded to Papa's
test rapping the table beside her crib or talking in a loud voice when her
head was turned by jerking her head or turning it, indicating that she
could hear as well as any baby should.

Having a baby around wasn't a totally new experience for Mom. She
had helped care for both Herb and Dick during her summers home from
the schools in Oakland and Berkeley. She didn't have to be taught the
fundamentals of child-care and she had plenty of time to devote to her
infant. Dad, on his part, loved gazing at the child, making faces at her,
touching her. In the evenings he held her and rocked her and gave her

her bottles. He was a proud, exuberant and resourceful father and he proved to be very ingenious in solving the problems that arose.

Like most babies, Donna was prone to awaken and cry when she was wet or hungry or uncomfortable. But when she awakened at night, neither Mom (who besides being deaf was a very sound sleeper) nor Dad could hear her, so Dad rigged up a string that he looped lightly around a slat in the crib so she couldn't tangle herself in it, and tied it to his thumb. When Donna tossed restlessly or, fussed because she was uncomfortable, her movements would cause the string to jerk Dad's thumb and he would wake up.

"That's marvelous!" Gram remembered exclaiming when she first heard of the device. Papa, appreciative but amused, asked what Dad did once he was awake. He grinned and signed *I push Mildred until she gets up to take care of the baby!*

Mom and Dad again attracted the attentions of curiosity seekers at church, as they had when they'd been married, but the focus of attention was short-lived. The baby behaved like any other baby and her parents like any other new parents. As the first grandchild, Donna was bounced from one set of admiring arms to another. Dad, of course, loved being in the limelight and couldn't resist bragging how beautiful his new daughter was.

Gram, quietly and unobtrusively, continued to keep tabs on how Mom was doing. She drove out to pick up her and the baby to take them to Willows for bi-monthly check-ups by the doctor. She knitted and quilted and sewed and made trips to the grocery store and dairy. She kept aware of such things as Mom's supply of diapers and how to obtain a stronger medicated cream for rash from the druggist. She helped Mom make furniture covers and to shop for things that she needed around the house. Many times she bought these items with her own money, for Mom didn't always have the change—or didn't remember to ask Dad for housekeeping money. "It was always a difficulty for her," Gram once described Mom's handling of money. "She's never had to fend for herself and Avo paid all of the major bills. Neither she nor your Dad seemed to worry about the little details. They always had been taken care of by someone else, I guess, and your parents assumed they would be taken care of in the future." Gram even took care of the comments made by people in the community. One comment was made by a woman who approached Gram and asked, "Mildred isn't going to have any more children is she?" Very surprised by the question, Gram looked at her with her wide eyes and stated, "Now I have no control over that!"

Donna, a fat, happy, spoiled "little rascal" with curly brown hair and dark eyes "made all the worry and fear and uncertainty that had gone into raising Mildred worthwhile" as far as Gram was concerned. I have a snapshot of Mom sitting in a lawn chair holding Donna when she was four or five months old. It very identifiably is a '50's picture—Mom's hair is short, in a permanent; Dad standing beside her with one arm around her shoulder, is crewcut and wearing a clean white t-shirt and jeans. Donna, in a sun dress, has her toes curled and one pudgy fist raised.

Perhaps she knew what was in store for her—or sensed it. Donna once told me that she didn't know whether she had "—been raised by Mom and Dad or whether I raised them." As the hearing, speaking child of two deaf parents, she was to become the family spokes-person, a miniature adult whose responsibilities far outstretched her authority. Sometimes it was very difficult for her. "To say the least," I remember her laughing, "I had a very unique childhood."

Had she remained an only child, she more easily might have bounced along in her own little world, precocious and self-sufficient, her father's darling and her grandparents' delight, close to them but with time of her own to be a little girl. Unfortunately for her, Mom soon became pregnant again. The son that Dad had expected—and wanted—now was on its way. *One of each!* he laughingly told friends and relatives, pointing first to Mom, then to himself *A pretty one like her and a strong one like me!*

On June 28, 1953, Mom delivered her second child, a bright-eyed, wide-faced, dark-haired girl that they named Peggy Jeanne. So open had Dad been, so hopeful and naively certain that this would be his son, he stuttered and shrugged and tried to hide his chagrin when Gram relayed the news from the nurse. But being basically good-humored, and a realist who loved children, he recovered, again joking to his in-laws *Okay, but just wait. The next one, for sure, will be a boy! For absolutely sure!*

The "next one," born two-and-a-half years later in the same hospital room, was me. And when Dad learned that, again, he had been denied a son, he cried. The nurse on duty came away shocked. "He actually cried!" she told Gram. Conciliatory as always, Gram nodded and smiled and told her that Dad would get over it, that he had two girls already and had been hoping for a boy.

But he never did get over it. Hardly a family gathering passes, scarcely do I make a visit to my parents, that he mentions it and apologizes. *I didn't mean it* he signs. Or *I'm sorry I cried when you were born—I love you.* And I laugh and sign back to him *I know you do. You don't have to say you're sorry.* But even as I do, I know he'll bring it up again. He felt that embarrassed about it.

Within a year after I was born, Mom became pregnant again. As she had with we three older girls, she moved in with Gram for the last couple of weeks before the baby was due. We kids were farmed out to various relatives and Dad often stayed over with the Carrieres to be near Mom. He was there, asleep in the bunk house, when his first son, my brother Gary, was born.

Gram called the house and Mom's brother Herb answered the phone.

Herb was then seventeen, a lively, good-spirited youngster in his senior year of high school. "Okay, sure, I'll tell Henry," he assured Gram, went out to the bunk house and shook Dad awake.

Mildred just had her baby! he told Dad in sign. *It's another girl!*

"He just looked at me and blinked," Herb laughed. "Then he waved his hand in disgust, turned over and went back to sleep!"

Hand cupped over his mouth to keep from laughing, Herb rushed out of the bunk house and went back into the house. He clapped his hands, laughed, checked the time, fixed himself a sandwich and grabbed a couple of cookies out of the tin Gram always kept in the kitchen, then went back to the bunk house. Dad grunted and waved him away when Herb tried to wake him up again, but Herb was insistent.

I was kidding he confessed, a wide grin on his face. *It's not a girl. This time it's a boy!*

"I never saw anyone move so fast in my life!" Herb remembered. "I think your Dad was out of the house and into his car and downtown passing out cigars before I even got back into the livingroom. If anybody ever set any Olympic records, he did it that day. He literally was in orbit. It took him weeks to settle down!"

At last Dad had what he wanted most: a son who could play baseball, and football, and run track. And, as it turned out, he was blessed not with just one son, but three. Two years after Gary's birth, Mom brought Rick into the world and two years after that my youngest brother Steve was born. *Three of each!* Dad bragged, passing out cigars for the last time. *Three pretty ones like Mildred and three strong ones like me!*

CHAPTER VII

"Janet!"

Her voice was sharp, preemptory. I knew something was wrong. Slowly I turned, resisting the impulse to pretend I didn't hear her and dart off. "What do you want?" I mouthed the words petulantly.

"Where are you going?"

My lips tightened. I wanted to look her in the eye but couldn't. "To Joy's house," I mumbled.

Hands on her hips, she stood facing me. Cross-examining me. Had I made my bed? How late was I going to stay? Did I have Joy's mother's permission? Finally, released to do what I wanted to do, I skipped down the sidewalk, muttering under my breath Oh! What a bully! Someday I'll get even!

Looking back on that scene and others very much like it, I wonder what a stranger passing through town might have thought of those two little girls, the younger one on the bottom step of the big house's porch, her hands pudged into fists and her lower lip protruding, and the other, her sister, on the top step, arms folded and a frown prematurely creasing her nine-year-old's brow? They must not have a mother . . . he might have concluded. Or the mother is ill and the nine-year-old temporarily is taking her place.

But Mom wasn't ill. And my older sister Donna hadn't taken her place. She had, however, become the family spokesperson. She, not my Mom, decided where-and when-I could spend the night with friends. For, you see, she could hear and talk. She could deal with my friends' mothers. And she could enforce rules conveyed by spoken command.

Throughout my childhood, Donna functioned as a second mother. She did not choose the role willingly: it was thrust upon her almost from the moment of her birth. People who could not talk to Mom or Dad soon learned that they could relay messages through their talking, hearing, oldest child—either personally, or by telephone. Gram could call and give Donna instructions. Uncle John and Avo could leave messages for Dad instead of driving over to the house to talk to him directly. The mothers of our friends called her, not Mom, to corroborate their daughters' plans, or to find out where their daughters were.

Even Dad's creditors called Donna to check on payments. If we wanted something picked up or delivered, Donna gave the clerk at the store, or the dispatcher at the Greyhound station, or the trash man, the necessary instructions. Gradually, as she grew older, she assumed many of the responsibilities that Gram had handled when Mom was growing up.

With this responsibility went power. As the third in line, subject to her commands and whims, I thought Donna was "stuck up" and "bossy." I didn't realize what a load she was carrying, or how quickly compared to the rest of us she had had to grow up. As it was for all of us children, sign was Donna's first language; English her second. She was, according to Mom and Gram, a precocious child, eager and active. Unfortunately, nobody in Glenn County knew how to teach the hearing child of deaf parents how to handle the situations that confronted her. So Mom and Dad, and Gram, and Uncle John and his wife Aunt Patsy, played it by ear. They protected Donna when they thought she needed protecting, scolded her when she needed scolding, and gave her free reign when she indicated that she could handle what was going on.

Handle it she did. In appearance and attitude, she was an ordinary enough little girl, with idiosyncracies and aspirations like those of most of her playmates and schoolmates. She made mud pies, climbed trees, dressed her dolls and ate ice cream with the best of her generation.

But she also grew up in a world without language as most children of her age and generation knew it. As a talking child, she had to learn herself at a very young age. Margene, who lived just across the levee from the Carrieres, remembered Donna translating for Mom and Dad in a grocery store when she was only two. Her facility for speech did not extend to reading, however.

Gram remembered that one of the nuns assigned to Saint Monica's Church in Willows telephoned her concerning Donna. "Donna was in the first grade at the time, and was enrolled in a catechism class at the church. Apparently the nun had told Donna that she wanted to talk to her parents and Donna, after explaining that they were deaf, had given her my name.

"You know that Donna is failing in her prayers?" the nun said. I was shocked: Donna was such a bright child—I couldn't feature her failing at anything. I drove over and talked to her. The assignments involved the memorization of certain prayers. I had Donna get her books out and asked her to read the prayers to me. Only then did I realize that Donna couldn't read!"

Both Mom and Dad could read—but they only could talk about what they read in sign. They couldn't sit around a table in the evening, as many parents did, point to the big letters in magazine ads or on newspaper headlines, and say "A" and "N" and "Z" and "boy" and "girl" and "cat" and get their child to imitate them. Donna simply had no early childhood reading experiences to relate to when she started going to school. Reading was a mystery to her—such a mystery that she couldn't even ask for help.

"Well! We'll just have to do something about this!" Gram decided. She arranged to drive to our house every week, before Donna's catechism lesson, and go over the prayers with her. Donna, eager and bright, soon learned them and before long a gold star appeared beside her name on the Honor Roll of the Month that the nuns posted on a bulletin board near the front of the church.

"I was really excited," Donna remembered. "It was like telling everybody, Boy! You're top dog! You did it! You made it!' and that really was important to me."

Both Peggy and I took the catechism classes when we entered the first grade and we also won gold stars. But it wasn't the same big deal, for we had no problems learning the prayers. Donna was there to help us. Donna taught us to say "A" and "N" and "Z" and read words like "cat" and "fork" and "dog." She did for us what Gram had done for her—and that established a pattern that continued throughout Peggy's and my separate girlhoods.

As Donna grew older, Gram relied on her to do many of the things that Gram always had done for Mom. Because they could communicate by telephone, the two of them arranged everything from cleaning the house for special events to purchasing the school supplies we younger children needed. In addition, Donna went shopping with Mom to translate sign into English and English into sign. Once she told me that one of her most constant recollections from childhood is the sight of someone bending over to face her. Tell your Mommy . . . he or she is saying . . . that what she needs to do is. . . .

"I answered the telephone so often that I shiver every time it rings, even now," she told me recently. "It was difficult explaining the calls to Dad and Mom. Often I couldn't even understand what the people who were calling were talking about. Then, when I'd tell Dad, he wouldn't understand my translation. He'd laugh, or shake his head, or wave his hand and I wouldn't know what to do. Sometimes the person on the other end of the line would get mad. I'd want to break down and just cry."

Once, she recalled, the TV set conked out. With some trepidation, she called the repairman.

"What's wrong with it?" he wanted to know.

"It's broke," Donna told him.

"Well, what's . . . hey, lemme talk to your Mom or Dad."

"They can't hear you. They're deaf."

"Okay. Just tell me what's wrong with the set. Does it light up when you turn it on?"

"Yes."

"Is the horizontal line moving?"

Silence.

"What . . . what is a horace—?" Donna gritted her teeth and clenched her little fist. "I don't know what that is! All I know the T.V.'s broke and my Dad wants you to come out and fix it. . . ."

Years later she admitted, "I didn't know what people like that expected of me. They confused me. I felt a lot of pressure."

Despite the pressure, however, Donna did have a great deal of support. She turned to Gram when she needed help, and Mom and Dad always were home—as they were throughout the time that I was growing up. They provided a very secure, comfort-giving, family-centered home life. They seldom went anywhere without us and, within our family, they were warm and sharing and comfortable to be around. Unlike some of his contemporaries, Dad didn't take off for hours when nobody knew where he was. As kids, we three girls seldom—if ever—were left alone. We all felt secure and very well cared for.

When I was six or seven, Dad and Mom moved into a big two-story house located next to the fire station in Willows. Avo, as always handled all the details. With its big backyard, big cheerful rooms and upstairs bedrooms, it proved to be a great place for kids to grow up. We could walk to school, and the downtown stores; we could invite our friends over— virtually hold open house, for Mom and Dad, unlike many of our friend's parents, loved the helter-skelter activities of children, and, of course, weren't bothered by the noise we made.

I know that the parents of many of our friends thought our family lived a confused and disordered life. Mom and Dad didn't set down rules and we made our own decisions and kept our own hours. "It's a wonder we didn't run wild!" Donna sat in my kitchen one evening and shook her head. "We could have, you know."

But we didn't. As I said, we were a close family—a solid family, secure and loving, and our Catholic religious background was very strong. Mom and Dad trusted us so implicitly that setting curfews, or investigating where we went, or who we associated with, never occurred to them. Trust that deep sets firmer boundaries than hard-and-fast rules or spankings ever could.

There were, also, disadvantages. Out of the security of that home we stepped into a world filled with words. When we were upset or discouraged or confused, we couldn't go to our parents the way other children could. Mom and Dad would hug us, and help us, and hold us when we were hurt, but they couldn't vocalize some of the things that we felt we needed. Our questions often drew only flitting responses. They could not answer many of our questions, nor could they share those accomplishments and joys that only words can convey.

Their inability to grasp subtle emotional issues often confused us. As children we'd get exasperated trying to explain school pranks, difficult assignments or taunting words from other children. We had to learn to deal with them ourselves. Donna, in those moments, was the key, the facilitator, the "little mother" who could sift through complicated needs to give or get permission or to complete school assignments or to define importances.

Situations that would have been problems for our schoolmates sometimes became big problems for us. For instance, Donna came home one evening and found that she was locked out of the house. She knocked and knocked—but of course neither Mom nor Dad could hear her. Both Peggy and I were asleep and she couldn't awaken us. Finally, Donna tromped to a neighbor's house and asked to use their telephone. She dialed our number and let the phone ring until Peggy finally woke up.

"Peggy!" Donna rasped, "Go downstairs and unlock the door. I can't get in!"

Donna was invited to her first birthday party when she was four or five years old. She remembered liking it "—a lot!" By the time she was in school, the parents of most of her friends had started giving their daughters and sons little parties on their birthdays. "That was neat— having all those kids over, getting all those presents," Donna recalled. Mom couldn't organize an event like that: had she been asked to, she wouldn't have known how to go about it since, throughout her life, Gram had made such arrangements for her. So Donna, always spunky and able to take charge, organized her own birthday party.

We were still living in the country then. As Gram told it, Donna did the whole thing herself. She picked the date and time, made the invitations, bought the cake and ice cream and decorated the livingroom. She selected the party favors and acted both as guest and hostess. Once the kids started to arrive, Mom was delighted and helped out. But she never could have arranged it herself.

"Boy! I must have been a real dandy!" Donna looked back on those days. "Planning my own parties and everything."

"Well Donna," I told her, "you did what you thought was right. You did it because you wanted a party and you knew that the only way it was going to get done was if you did it yourself."

Almost invariably, Dad and Mom and Gram backed Donna when she took the initiative. Donna planned and supervised Peggy's and my parties, too. Once, when Donna was older—probably in her early teens— a friend's mother called Gram.

"Your granddaughter Donna is having a party."

"Yes, I heard."

"But it's a slumber party!"

"Well," Gram retorted, "it's her party, isn't it?"

As far as Gram was concerned, Donna could handle the situation. No one needed to interfere.

Usually no one did. But once in a while Donna would exceed her bounds. Her independence made her bossy and Peggy and I resented being ordered around. Harriet Wampler described Donna as "—a smarty-pants—" and Aunt Patsy told me, "She thought she could do anything she wanted to do. You couldn't say no to her."

Gram once taught her a lesson. When Gram's sister Marie passed away, Mom and Dad went with Gram to the San Francisco Bay Area for the funeral. We kids were farmed out to Gram's neighbor Margene. Donna, by her own admission, got "—prissy and smarty—" and Margene, a no-nonsense type of woman, scolded her for it.

Donna wasn't used to that kind of treatment and got mad. She decided Margene was mean and convinced herself that Margene shouldn't be taking care of her. Gram, she pouted, should have known better.

When Gram telephoned to check on how everybody was doing, she asked each of us what little gifts we wanted from the city. When Donna's turn to talk to her came, and Gram asked her what she wanted, Donna shot back, "Nothing! I don't want anything!"

Gram cautioned her to behave and told her to tell us that she and Mom and Dad would be home the next day. As promised, they picked us up at Margene's and we went over to Gram's for supper. Gram had little gifts for everyone . . . except Donna.

"Where's mine?" Donna asked, her voice quavering.

"You said you didn't want anything," Gram replied evenly, "so I didn't buy anything for you."

"That was such a shock!" Donna recalled years later. "I couldn't believe that I didn't get anything—I just couldn't believe it!" And, she added, "That was a lesson that stuck with me for the rest of my life. I tried never to respond that way again— particularly with Gram."

Donna's cockiness and sassiness was partly a defense mechanism. The adult world that she had to deal with often was demanding and hostile. By the time I entered the first grade, Dad already had been working for Avo for seven or eight years. A great deal of the management of the dairy and the surrounding farmland that Avo owned or controlled had fallen on John's shoulders and Donna often had to deal with him concerning bills, purchases and other minor financial matters.

Most of our family's major purchases and payments—for cars, appliances, fuel bills, etc.—went through John and Avo. But as the children of long-time respected local residents, Dad and Mom could charge things at local stores. I presume that these stores mailed monthly statements to us at home and that Dad tossed them aside. Perhaps he didn't understand them, or didn't understand what they were for; quite possibly he presumed that John or Avo would take care of them.

As independent an individual as he was, and as insistent as he was that he could function on his own, Dad never showed much interest in money or setting up budgets. As a boy, he seldom had to worry about money, and

Avo didn't often discuss the internal workings of his finances with him. As far as Dad could tell, Avo always had enough cash available. Like many farmer-businessmen, Avo wasn't tied to a monthly salary. He had reserves, borrowing power, land and other assets and bought and sold according to the market, his needs and—sometimes—his whims. And while Dad correctly understood that, as Avo's son, partner and employee, he could claim some of the business's income, he didn't seem to know exactly what that consisted of in terms of dollars and cents. Unlike a factory or office employee, he couldn't sit down and thumb through paycheck stubs knowing that they represented his purchasing power for the month.

More than once, the repercussions from this cavalier attitude that Dad had about payments and bills fell on Donna's shoulders. Gram remembered taking Donna into a department store one Saturday in late summer. The store bookkeeper saw them and rushed out and confronted Donna, who was only eight or nine years old at the time. "Why hasn't your father paid this bill?" the bookkeeper demanded.

Donna backed away, startled and confused. "I—I don't know," she mumbled.

"Well, you tell him to come in and pay it." The bookkeeper whirled and stalked back to her office in the back of the store.

Gram was so startled she didn't know what to say. "Oh! but it sure burned me up!" she remembered. "And I felt so sorry for poor Donna. The woman should have known it wasn't Donna's fault. Had she just come up and told us about the problem in a nice way, I could have taken care of it. Your father certainly wasn't intentionally trying to cheat the store out of anything."

Dad's laxness with money matters led to some altercations with his brother John. Aunt Patsy told me that Dad's failure "to take more responsibility" about such things created problems when we were kids. John may have questioned Dad about the department store bill and/or other little unpaid accounts like it and in the process may have hurt Dad's feelings. Dad—as stubborn as Avo when he set his mind on something—probably reacted by refusing to open business mail sent to our house. This reaction, in turn, upset Aunt Patsy. "He just brought the bills over to our house and dumped them in our laps," she told me.

John may have questioned Dad about the bill. . . . There's more to that phrase than meets the eye. Had it been Frankie, not Dad, that John had questioned about an unpaid bill he would have given him a straight forward answer. Even if it had angered one or the other of them, each would have been able to gauge, by tone of voice and choice of words, what stance the other was taking. With the deaf, subtleties like that fall by the wayside. Only a thin line separates "questioning" from "criticizing" and that thin line is difficult to accurately express in the language of the deaf, especially when tempers are flaring.

Equally difficult for the deaf is trying to explain what motivates a particular act or action. Dad easily could describe what he'd done at any given time, whether it was on the farm, on the ball field or at home. Why he'd done it was more of a problem, particularly if it involved a purchase or action that was an exception to the norm. John, or Avo, or even one of us kids, might ask *Why did you buy that?* and Dad would reply, *I needed it!*

But what a big word *need* is! For example, someone may "need" to wash the dishes, they may "need" a new toaster, they may "need" to lose weight, they may "need" comforting because their best friend has died, they may "need" to make love. To pursue such questioning with someone who has been born and grown up deaf may only confuse them. *Henry, why did you need that?* John could ask and Dad might frown, shake his head, get irritated. If the subject were new shoes, he could point to a hole in his old ones. But if the subject were something less tangible, he could only repeat *I needed it!* and become annoyed if John insisted on pursuing the subject.

These breakdowns in communication frequently put Donna at odds with Aunt Patsy. She would want to know why something hadn't been done and go to Donna rather than Dad or Mom because she knew that she could talk to Donna. Almost invariably, Donna would get defensive—or "smarty-pantsy." She would stick up for Dad and refuse to listen to Aunt Patsy. Donna wasn't alone in this reaction; both Peggy and I, and later Gary and the younger boys, shared it. We knew what good people our parents were and we didn't want anybody inferring that they didn't do the things that they should do. Quite to the contrary, we thought other parents could have taken lessons from them.

Not that we were always right. Nor that Donna never stepped on toes herself. As she grew older, she assumed more and more household responsibilities. She made sure that Peggy, Gary, Rick, Steve and I, were properly outfitted for school, for church, for work and play. One fall she bought shoes for all of us. She insisted that we select sturdy, comfortable footwear—nothing fancy, impractical or exorbitant. Having no money herself, she charged them at the shoe store.

Aunt Patsy hit the roof. Years later I learned why. "I had been paying for a pair of shoes for my son Mark and was waiting for payday to buy a pair for Shiela. You guys went down and charged all of yours—a pair for school and a Sunday pair for each of you—and Shiela almost had to do without. I don't blame Donna— she thought she was doing the right thing. It's just that she could do things like that and I couldn't. It made me mad."

I suppose, like Donna, Aunt Patsy was hyper-conscious about the responsibilities she felt that she had taken on. In her case, they weren't precisely thrust on her, however. As she told me, "I can remember when Johnny and I made the decision to get married that one of the discussions was that did I understand that Henry and Mildred would always be part of our lives and part of our responsibilities—always! And I accepted that."

Her perception of the relationship between Dad and his brother, and between the two of them and Avo, differed from the one I usually heard expressed in our family. We often felt that Uncle John's family got everything they wanted, while we had to beg and badger and justify and cajole to get anything at all.

"No," Aunt Patsy insisted. "Whenever Johnny fought Avo for something, he was fighting for Henry and Mildred at the same time. In my mind, Avo many, many years ago, in his own mind and for his own convenience, actually gave Henry to Johnny. Henry and Mildred and you kids have always been a part of our marriage, since you were very, very young."

"There were so many things you kids couldn't do," she noted. "Grandma Enos couldn't do much to help Henry and your family and so that share of activity fell upon my shoulders. We knew that Henry and Mildred weren't educated in things like keeping accounts and keeping track of money and we were hoping, as you got older, that you kids would help them with these things."

Which, of course, we did. Perhaps, in the process of assuming those responsibilities, we—or, specifically, Donna—didn't perceive how much Uncle John and Aunt Patsy were doing, or that they were in fact looking out for our best interests, and not just their own.

For all his emotionality, and his demonstrativeness, Dad can be cold and offhanded when it comes to expressing appreciation or giving thank-you's, particularly when the service for which the thanks is owed isn't obvious or immediately visible. And Uncle John, like Avo, often hides behind a gruff and business-like mien, waiting for an expression of appreciation which never comes. As he told me:

"As we go through life in this partnership we have, I've wondered if Henry appreciates what I've done. He takes so much for granted; I get no satisfaction for having helped him. Yet if I pulled the pin, it would be hard for him to stand alone. He wouldn't know where to begin."

The issue of "responsibility" arises whenever I talk to Uncle John and Aunt Patsy about Dad. Aunt Patsy, in particular, faults Dad for not taking enough initiative around the dairy. "I think there are lots of things that Henry could do that he chooses not to do. He's smart, but he chooses to show his intelligence only when it's convenient. And John claims that Avo and Grandma Enos "spoiled" Dad. "It was like a babysitter taking care of your kids all day. Then when you return, all you have to do is put them to bed. That's the way Henry's going to school worked, as far as I was concerned. He was gone so much that when he came home, Mom and Dad spoiled him."

Dad's stubbornness is hard to deal with. Often, however, John laughs it off. "He's just like Avo. When someone disagrees with Avo, he just turns around and leaves. Then he does what he pleases whether you like it or don't. Henry's the same way, only that to "listen" he has to look at you."

And, he adds, so was Avo's, father. "Let's face it, stubbornness is a Portuguese trait!"

Unfortunately this quality in Avo, this tendency to make erratic sometimes presumptuous decisions, to give orders without regard to questions or conditions, and try to dominate by sheer force of personality, works to both Dad's and Uncle John's disadvantage. But over the years, John has developed a patient, effective managerial attitude. As he said, "Avo makes some decision, I make some—others we talk about. Usually the final decision, I make, especially if it involves purchasing something."

In his own mind, he's never attempted to short-change Dad or cut him out of anything that is owed to him. "Here's the way it works," he explained one evening at his house. "I was already working on the ranch before I got married. Avo called the shots and Henry and I would go along with what he said. Frank was in and out of the picture. As time went on, and Avo was getting older, Avo did less of the actual physical work. He became more or less the P.R. man. As a result, the responsibilities for making decisions—a lot of them are day to day and have be made spontaneously—shifted to me."

"But I never considered your Dad as anything other than a partner. I always figured that whatever happened, happened to both of us. If we're broke, we're broke together. The problem is, whenever you have a family working together, you're going to have some problems. When it's difficult to communicate, as it is between Henry and me, it's hard to resolve those differences. Even if you think you have resolved them, sometimes all you've done is smooth things over on the surface. You don't really get rid of it."

Perhaps had either Donna or Peggy or I known what we know now, we could better have understood the opposition we felt that we got from Uncle John and Aunt Patsy. But we were children. Nobody explained finances to us, or why we had to wait for a new refrigerator, or why our cousins had new clothes and we didn't. Instead we formed theories of our own, and sometimes reacted towards our Enos relatives as though they were our enemies.

Donna's interchanges with the Enos family were not limited to quarreling over bills. Nor were they confined to Uncle John and Aunt Patsy. She also had to deal with the sometimes entangled relationships among

Avo and his brothers. Avo, assertive and success-oriented, had aroused their ire with some of his land dealings. As young men, the four brothers, Avo, Manuel, Joe and Tony, had been fairly close. But after their father died, the brothers disagreed over some of the property settlements and their relationships became less cordial and somewhat strained.

My Uncle Joe, the second youngest of the brothers, was taciturn—almost surly. He kept to himself and often would stalk past his nephews without speaking to them. John remembered seeing him walk the ditch-line, a spade over his shoulder, and neither nod nor blink despite being addressed.

This type of treatment upset Dad, who was ebullient and outgoing and wanted everyone to like him. As John described it, "Your Dad always was sensitive to slights." According to John, "Joe probably ignored Henry more than anyone else. I suppose he didn't want to bother with sign language. Your Dad would get his hackles up every time Joe stalked past him without speaking, waving or even acknowledging a greeting."

One night, when Donna was only eight or nine years old, Dad and Joe got in an altercation during a big Portuguese Festa. Three or four times a year, following the traditions of the Old Country, Portuguese families from throughout the area would get together to eat, drink, talk and dance. Earlier that week, Dad and Joe had argued over something involving the borders between their separate properties—perhaps to do with irrigation, or fencing, or cutting across each other's land. When they crossed paths at the Festa, the argument resumed.

Dad—energetic, out-going, easily excited—began waving his hands. Joe, like so many men of Portuguese descent, was voluble and de-monstrative when aroused. He shoved Dad—perhaps in retaliation as Dad pushed up close to him—and Dad yelled and shoved back. When he's angry, Dad's voice rises and though he doesn't form words, his vocaliza-tions are intense and frightening. Joe, though older than Dad, was strong and farm-toughened; he clenched his fists and the two of them went at it, their mutual frustrations erupting into a flurry of haymakers.

Onlookers rushed in to separate them. One of Dad's blows broke Joe's glasses and may have cut his face. He was still shouting at Dad as he was pulled away. Someone bent over him to examine his face. Dad tried to free himself to get another crack at Joe. He almost succeeded but more peacemakers intervened.

The minute that the fight started, someone called the sheriff's office. A patrol car sped to the scene. The two deputies questioned the onlookers and Joe but, of course, they couldn't talk to Dad. Joe's version of the set-to made it seem that Dad was at fault. Since most of the argument had been conducted in sign, no one at the Festa could accurately describe what it was about.

Donna had gone to the Festa with Dad, although Mom and the rest of us had not. No one told the deputies that she would be stranded if they took Dad to jail. "I felt horrible!" she remembered. "I was scared to death!" Finally Manuel came over and told Donna that he and Inez would take her home.

As soon as Donna got inside the house, she called Avo. "I could barely talk," she remembered. "I was kind of scared of Avo anyway, and he kept asking me questions that I couldn't answer. All I knew was that Dad was in jail and nobody seemed to care what had happened to him."

Avo called John, then went to get Dad. Evidently, Avo's explanation of what had happened, both at the Festa and before, satisfied the authorities, for they released Dad without filing any charges against him. Donna, however, had nightmares about the incident for years.

The incident stands out in my mind because it illustrated so well how Donna was pressed into situations that forced her to react as an adult despite her age. And it so dramatically demonstrated how unsympathetic the hearing world could be with Dad. The deputies who came in to break up the fight couldn't understand him. As far as they were concerned, he was some kind of mad man who could only wave his arms and make funny noises, or a carouser who'd imbibed far too much liquor and was showing the effects of it with his voice and his fists. They believed what Joe told them because Joe could talk, even though the responsibility for starting the fight was unknown to them.

Throughout my life, I've known that Dad's deafness has made it difficult for him to deal with his father and brothers. Their misunderstandings generally have been attributed to his lack of hearing, his inability to understand directions, his lack of conventional education. Yet Avo and his brothers, though able to speak to each other and hear each other, couldn't always handle their own relationships without contention. They had no physical obstacles like deafness to impair them. Was it really Dad's deafness that created all the misunderstandings?

Deafness, I've noticed, sometimes can be an excuse, one often used by those in the hearing world to pass over or get around a more subtle—but no less obvious—failing in themselves.

As our "little mother," as the first "talking Enos" in our family, Donna was capable and efficient. She was not by any means a prune-faced, dour little child, however. Though "bossy" to Peggy and me, she had many friends and was fun-loving, outgoing and popular. By taking responsibilities, she earned her own freedoms—set her own deadlines, her own curfews, her own limits and sometimes ours. As oldest sister, appearance conscious and popular in school, she also assumed certain privileges— particularly the right to wear her two sisters' best clothes.

"Oh! I used to get frantic phone calls from Peggy," Gram laughed as she told me her impressions of our family when we were young. "'Gram!' she'd plead, almost in tears, Donna's wearing my new dress!' I'd try to mollify her, say something like, Well, you girls need to share things, you know . . .' and Peggy would burst into tears. 'But Gram!' she'd wail, 'I haven't got to wear it yet myself!'"

When Donna and I first entered school, Gram would drive into town and go with us to enroll us. By the time the younger boys, Rick and Steve, were ready for the first grade, Donna had assumed that function. She walked, alone, to the county courthouse to obtain copies of their birth certificates, filled out the school papers and met the boys' teachers.

"I still remember the day she called to tell me, 'Gram, you don't have to go to any more parent-teacher conferences,'" Gram shook her head and laughed. "'I can take care of it from now on,' she said, just as mature as you please. And, from then on, she did in fact attend them. She was quite a little gal!'"

As the family grew, (six children in nine years is a considerable amount of growth!), its needs expanded and each of us, in our own way, took our share of the load. Donna, of course, bore the brunt of this growth and took on a tremendous amount of responsibility. Never, however, did she attempt to replace or usurp our mother, who remained the steady, loving, capable—if family-centered and shy—focal point around which our lives revolved. Donna, in effect, became an extension of Mom, doing for her those things which Mom couldn't do or would have had a great deal of trouble doing for herself. She continued to do many of these things even after she was in college—and later, married and beginning a family of her own. "I wonder sometimes whether they raised me or I raised them," she once laughed, looking back at our life with our parents.

I joined her in laughing. But privately I wondered how much more difficult my own life might have been had it not been for my "little mother."

CHAPTER VIII

I don't remember exactly what upset me at school that day. I only remember rushing home after the last bell rang, frustrated and hurt, my chest filling with sobs and my head aswirl with the way the world wronged me. I must have been fifteen then, impetuous and a bit chubby, a typical teenager overwhelmed by all the problems that teenagers throughout the world must face: metabolism changes, sudden bursts of insecurity: am I pretty? am I popular? why is everyone always picking on me? awareness of boys, and emotions that seemed to explode without warning. I hurried as fast as I could, a wad of kleenex in one hand, my purse in the other, and burst through the front door of our big house wanting to throw myself into my mother's arms and become her little girl again.

She was in the kitchen and didn't hear me. Just outside the kitchen doorway, I stopped. Aware of a presence—a change of vibrations in the house—she looked up, smiling. Then, seeing my expression, she frowned.

I whirled and cupped my face in my hands. She can't understand me! The realization cut through me like a knife. I felt hurt and betrayed—as though life itself had conspired against me. I desperately wanted to pour out my feelings to her, tell her everything that had happened to me and listen to wise and comforting words. She can't hear! She can't talk! She can't understand me! Before she could reach out to me, I turned and fled upstairs and flung myself across my bed.

"Why can't she hear? Why can't she hear?" I beat the pillows with my fist and shouted the words. Tears were pouring down my cheeks. "Why can't she hear?" I repeated at the top my voice.

As I gasped for breath I heard Mom's footsteps on the stairs. I choked back another outburst and lay face down on my bed, quivering and trembling. She hesitated in the doorway, then crossed the room and sat down on the bed beside me. Gently, lovingly, she began to rub my back. I closed my eyes. Then, slowly, I raised my head and turned to look at her. Impulsively, I grabbed her and squeezed her as tightly as I could. "I love you, I love you, Mom, I love you," I told her. That she couldn't hear me no longer mattered.

At least, for the moment, it no longer mattered. My parents' deafness was, at times, a definite problem for me—particularly when I was just entering my teens. Voluble and fun-loving, with a lot to say to anyone who would listen, I wanted to talk about my feelings, the day's events, my hopes—even my secrets. That I couldn't go to my mother with those impulses and express what I felt really tore me up inside.

I remember going to a friend's house one day after school. Some "big event" had happened—something to do with cheerleaders, or a Christmas pageant, or a field trip to Chico—and my friend, talking a mile a minute, described it to her mother. They both started laughing, snapping questions back and forth, making comments. Suddenly I felt very isolated, like a little girl watching a party she couldn't attend. My God!, I remember thinking, I've never talked to my mother that way!

Teenaged girls tend to feel sorry for themselves during their adolescence—certainly I was no exception. The gap in my life created by an unfilled need for a close vocal contact with my mother brought tears to my eyes and made me feel as though I were being deprived of something that all my schoolmates possessed. I wasn't mature enough at the time to perceive that many girls my age had apathetic—or even hostile—parents, were unloved—even rejected—and longed for a comfortable and secure home life like mine.

I suppose it is ironic that all of us Enos kids turned out to be so vocal. Ironic, but not surprising, for we grew up in a house filled with romping, good-natured rivalry and noise. The first home that I can remember was the farm that Avo bought for us in the country. In appearance, everything seemed chaotic: a fact that bothered visitors, particularly Uncle John and Aunt Patsy on one side of the family, and Gram on the other, a great deal. Mom, you see, didn't worry about unmade beds, piles of laundry, dirty dishes or scattered toys. Both she and Dad played with us, teased us, and laughed at our antics. Perhaps by choice, but more likely by instinct, they defined home life in terms of happiness, of having a good time. Unlike many of my friends' mothers, Mom didn't prize possessions more than she did her children. She wasn't constantly jumping up to protect things from our inquisitive fingers. Instead of *don't do this! don't do that!* it was down on the floor with us to snip with scissors, or into the kitchen to mix a bowl of cookie dough, or out in the yard to throw a ball or play hide-and-seek.

Those who haven't spent much time around deaf people assume that they live in a world without noise. Nothing could be farther from the truth. At gatherings of the deaf—particularly parties—the participants laugh and shout and bang things. Their language may not be coherent enough that an outsider can understand it, but that doesn't mean that it can't effectively communicate hilarity, effervescence and joy. The deaf are not by definition emotionless, joyless people who sit quietly in corners and spell out words with their fingers.

My Uncle Herb remembered some of the parties that Dad and Mom gave for their deaf friends shortly after they were married. Invited were old schoolmates like the Azevedo youth from Chico, the Wamplers, and others. "They made more noise than non-deaf people!" Herb laughed. "Every one of them had distinctive sound. Your Dad loved being the center of attention. He'd relive all of his athletic accomplishments. You could watch him and tell that he was swinging a bat or racing downfield with a football scoring the winning touchdown while everybody cheered."

Dad is truly emotional. When he was playing softball, we kids used to pile in the car and go to his game to watch. Coming home either was a romp or a gray and depressing experience, depending upon whether his team won or lost. I remember once, after an apparent victory for his team turned into a defeat, Gary and I huddled in the backseat trying not to move our lips as we whispered. Dad was so upset the car seemed to bristle with anger. Whether it was an umpire's call or an error that tipped the balance, I don't remember. But I do remember how long it seemed to take us to get home. No hearing, speaking person could have expressed his disappointment and frustration more vividly than Dad did that evening.

Donna, was my idol—as well as a constant thorn. Although her bossiness annoyed me, I envied and admired her freedom. As the youngest of three sisters, I felt that Donna, and often Peggy as well, got to do everything and I didn't get to do anything. I wanted desperately to go to school from the time that I was three or four years old. I can remember crawling upon the couch to peer over it and out the curtained window of the house on the farm to watch Donna and Peggy trot off to school.

One morning in particular sticks in my mind. It was raining very hard. My two sisters, shoulders hunched and heads tucked against their high coat collars, ran to catch the bus that stopped at the end of the gravel road leading to the highway. Even though the rain was pelting down, I envied them—how much fun it would be to be running off to catch that bus!

Just then Mom's hand touched my arms. I glanced up, surprised; she was smiling at Donna and Peggy. And, I realized, at me. I felt very warm inside and secure. And I realized without her saying anything in sign, that she understood what I felt. In my mind's eye, the heavy clouds and the driving rain suddenly became sunlight and calm. Mom could make me feel so good all over! I wonder now how I ever felt that her deafness was a handicap that deprived me in any way.

We moved from the house in the country to the house in town when I was six or seven years old. Willows, to my eyes, was a big, confusing city. How exciting all the varied activity seemed! The house, so big and comfortable looking, drew immediate approval. No longer would Donna and Peggy have to ride a bus and miss all the after-school activities. Mom now could walk to the stores—or send one of us if she needed something,. Dad, of course, would have to commute back and forth to work, but he had to do that from the farm anyway since Avo's holdings were so large.

Avo, John, Frank and Dad did most of the moving. Donna and Peggy helped carry boxes, sort and unpack; Gary, Rick and I got in the way more than anything else, but it was all for a good cause. Steve, still the baby, was in Mom's arms. We got table and chairs, beds and dressers set up and, despite protests from us young ones, we even took baths before we snuggled into bed for our first night in our new house.

Suddenly I leaped up, screaming. The loudest whistle I'd ever heard was rattling the window panes. Sirens throbbed against the walls. I stumbled out of bed and ran to the window. Donna and Peggy scrambled up beside me. "What's wrong? What's going on?" I shouted.

"It's a fire," Donna took a deep breath and shrugged one shoulder. If the noise had frightened her, she didn't show it. She pointed towards the fire engine careening out of the station house next door. Its flashing red lights flung weird-looking shadows across our faces and against the walls.

Gary, in the next room, was crying. Donna and I found him on the floor. The noise had startled him so badly he'd toppled out of bed and thumped his head on the floor. Donna picked him up and tucked him back into bed, describing what we'd seen and telling him that everything was okay. "We'll just have to get used to it, that's all," she said with the aplomb of a worldly and experienced sixth-grader.

It took us a while to get back to sleep. We were still talking about the sirens and engines the next morning when we got up and went downstairs to have breakfast. Mom wanted to know what we were so excited about. We told her and she shrugged. *I slept right through it* she told us. Of course, so did Dad. A little thing like fire whistles and sirens couldn't disrupt the sleep for the deaf.

We soon grew accustomed to such interruptions and either didn't wake up or merely rolled over and went back to sleep. Occasionally a friend spending the night with one or the other of us would jump up, alarmed, and we would laugh and poke fun at her for being so skittish. After all, living next to the fire station did have its advantages. There were no neighbors on that side of us to object to our running around and the lot surrounding the house was big enough to support a baseball diamond in the back yard and football field on the side lawn.

Kids from all over town banged in and out of the house, joining our games, our parties, our raids on the refrigerator. With their help, we built tree houses in the walnut trees in back and converted the old garage and storage shed into a hiding place, a clubhouse, a fort, and bleacher seats for the baseball games. "The Enos boys," a neighbor laughed, "didn't learn to walk, they learned to run the bases." He wasn't far from the truth. Gary, Rick and Steve started swinging bats when they were still in diapers. By the time they were in school, they were bashing home run drives over the garage.

Mom and Dad love kids—all kids, I think. As a pre-adolescent, I don't remember being self-conscious about their deafness—it was something I accepted and most of my friends quickly took it in stride. If anything, my parents' disability was a point in their favor, for they could tolerate amounts of noise that would drive other parents into fits of anger.

I think a lot of our friends came over just to cut loose, feel free, express themselves as all kids must, noisily and unself-consciously. In our house, record players blared—nobody objected if the volume was pushed as high as it would go. Kids could laugh, scream and yell and our parents didn't care. We could stay up later than most of our friends could, and we had more freedom of movement. It was all good clean fun and we never got into serious trouble—Donna saw to that, and Mom was always home to watch us. Often when Dad wasn't working, he'd join the games in the yard as an umpire or pitcher or quarterback. Had he not been deaf, he told me more than once, he would have gone on to college and become a coach. As far as many of my brother's friends were concerned, Dad talked with his curve ball or the long spiraling passes he could throw. To many of them, he was sort of a hero, the role model of what a father should be like. No wonder our house was always filled with laughter, racing footsteps, unfettered glee.

As disciplinarians, Mom and Dad were pushovers. Donna learned this quickly; so did Peggy and I. They were proud of us—more than that, they were proud of themselves for having so many active, healthy, hearing children—and this pride in us, this admiration of the things we did, made them permissive. As far as they were concerned, we could do no wrong. We came home at 10:00 o'clock, not 8:00 like most of our friends had to do. Donna's friends, in particular, periodically got in trouble with their parents for staying out too late. "How come Donna or Peggy, or Janet get to stay out late and I don't?" was a complaint voiced in many households. It never occurred to me to wonder at the time how those parents answered their daughters' and sons' complaints. Did they think less of my parents—and of us—because we were relatively undisciplined?

Somehow I doubt it. All of us were, after all, high achievers, both in school and on the playground. We were outwardly carefree, and did whatever we pleased, but we were a close-knit family and we looked out for each other. From earliest childhood, each of us assumed certain duties and responsibilities—our parents, we knew, needed us and we responded by becoming their ears and voices, their links to the world in which they lived.

This awareness, this understanding, came so instinctively that as young children, none of us questioned Mom's and Dad's deafness. Nor did we find it particularly unusual or unnatural. That's why outsiders' attitudes seemed so strange to us—we'd blink and frown at the way this or that friend's mother carried on. After all, weren't we taking care of everything? What in the world was the problem?

Because money was always available, and no one made any fuss about it, we older girls and Mom used to take whatever we needed for groceries, the drugstore or gas station from Dad's wallet. We always told him about it, and he'd smile and tell us that's what it was there for. Rick saw us do this, and understood that he could do the same thing if he really needed something and none of us was home to get it for him.

On his meandering around town, Rick went in and out of the local variety stores. One day he discovered a "G.I. Joe" outfit on sale there. It included helmet, gun, fatigues—the whole works. Rick really liked it. How many times he went back to inspect it—and picture himself wearing it—I don't know. But one day he decided that his need was great enough that he could take the money for the "G.I. Joe" outfit out of Dad's wallet.

Twenty dollars was a bigger sum that most of us took at any one time. Mom needed something for groceries and discovered that the $20 was gone. Dad didn't know what had happened to it; neither did any of us girls or Gary. We were in the process of looking behind furniture and under books and doilies when Rick strolled in, decked out like "G.I. Joe" from head to toe. "Oh boy!" Gary warned, "you're in for it!"

The poor kid! Dad was mad—but also amused. He let Rick know that he'd done the wrong thing—that wasn't what the money was there for—and Rick never forgot it. To this day, whenever I see a reference to "G.I. Joe" clothes or toys, I picture Rick decked out in that uniform. And I realize how open and trusting our parents were in their dealings with us as far as money was concerned.

One summer day, when I was nine or ten, I settled onto the porch steps with my doll to watch my brothers and sisters and a group of neighborhood friends play hide-and-seek. For some reason, I'd dropped out of the game, wanting, I suppose, to share a quiet and inturned moment with characters out of my imagination. I was in another world, a fantasy land of idyllic love and make-believe motherhood, when one of the older boys approached me.

"Hey! Hey, Janet!" His mouth curled into a taunting and malicious grin, "Hey! y'wanna know something?"

I frowned, half-turning—I was happy with my daydreams and didn't want him intruding upon them—but he grinned provokingly and insisted, "Hey, Janet! I want to tell you something!"

I straightened my shoulders and glared at him. He leaned towards me, his eyes gleaming. "Hey!" he continued, spacing the words carefully, like little darts he was throwing into my face, "you know what? Your parents aren't really deaf. They're only pretending!"

I blinked, startled and confused. What was he saying? I shook my head, starting to object, tell him that he was lying, but he bent closer.

"They're not really deaf. They're only pretending that they're deaf to see what you kids will try to get away with!"

I gasped, then lurched to my feet. "Don't say that!" I screamed, lunging towards him, "don't say that!"

"It's true! It's true!" he goaded me with his mocking laughter, "I heard them talking. I heard them say it!"

Still clutching my doll, I charged him, one fist clenched. I swung as hard as I could, but I missed and almost fell down. He laughed more loudly. He was half-again my size, broad-shouldered and tall; my head barely reached his chest. I swung again, as hard as I could, and hit him square in the stomach.

The blow didn't faze him. "They're not deaf!" he laughed as I swung and hit him again. Tears were pouring out of my eyes—I couldn't restrain them. Nor did I want to. I just kept swinging and hitting him, crying and yelling, "You're wrong! You're wrong!"

He put his hand against my head and laughed. I couldn't hit him hard enough to hurt him but I wouldn't stop swinging. The hide-and-seek game broke up and all the other kids, including my sisters and brothers, ran over to see what was happening. They formed a circle around us. I kept swinging and hitting and crying and shouting until I couldn't stand up any longer. My shoulders slumped; I looked up at him. He was still taunting, laughing, telling those vicious lies. I swung one more time, then, still clutching my doll as tightly as I could, I whirled and broke through the circle of kids and ran up the stairs into the house.

"He's wrong, he's wrong," I sprawled across my bed and continued to sob. Finally Donna came in to talk to me. "He's a nasty boy. You know he was lying," she told me and I nodded. But her words didn't assuage the wound his words had opened. It was not what he said, but what his words implied, that had hurt me so much. I knew my parents were deaf—that was an undisputable fact. But I'd never before realized that lies could be told about them, or that anyone who'd visited our house and played with us could say anything that wasn't praiseworthy about them.

I didn't go to Gram with that particular incident, but I went to Gram often with questions and problems. She was a constant presence—both physically and spiritually. For nearly thirty years she had taken care of Mom—almost literally attended to her every need. She quietly— unassumingly but effectively—transferred this attention to Donna, Peggy and me. We became, as it were, the talking daughters she always had wanted.

As she always had insisted that Mom be "special" and above reproach, she insisted that Mom's daughters never do anything that would embar- rass their deaf mother. We weren't afraid of Mom and Dad, but we were, in a peculiarly loving way, afraid of Gram. She held us in such high esteem from the time that we were infants that we didn't dare do, or say, or become involved in, anything that would cause this esteem to be withheld or withdrawn.

"Oh, Janet! What would Gram say?" was the most intimidating de- terrent that Donna could give. Hearing it, I'd wince, or bite my lip and retrace my steps—like Donna and Peggy, I wanted to be a good girl as Gram thought that I was. When a teacher threatened to give me a low grade because I didn't turn in homework, or was cutting up in class, the phrase What would Gram think? straightened me out. It appeared whenever I was tempted to cut a class or date someone I shouldn't or make a nasty remark. Mom and Dad I could handle, but Gram . . . I simply couldn't, or wouldn't do anything that might hurt Gram!

She was both tactful and sensible. She never intruded and seldom voiced any disapproval, either of what I or my sisters did or what Mom and Dad did. She was old enough to be objective and sympathetic about many things that either tempted or confused us. I remember picking up the phone and calling her about vexing teenagers' problems that I couldn't explain to Mom.

Soon after I started junior high school, I noticed that some girls my age were starting to wear nylons. I tried some on— perhaps they were Donna's—but couldn't decide whether or not they looked "right" on me. I needed advice—I wanted to look grown-up, but I didn't want to be conspicuous or look silly—and I couldn't go to Mom. Like I said, she was a pushover: she would have shrugged and signed that if I wanted to wear them, I could. So I called Gram.

"Some of the girls are wearing nylons," I explained. "Do you think it would be all right if I wore them?"

Gram's laugh was indulgent—almost caressing. "Well, Janet, I don't know. Have you tried some on?"

"Yes."

"What did you think?"

"Well, Gram, I don't. . . . I mean, I'm not sure, they look kind of . . . different."

Again Gram laughed. "Then probably it's too soon, Janet. Why don't you wait a year or two? Then you can start wearing them to church, and on special occasions."

As I hung up the phone, I remember giving a little sigh of relief. Though I wanted nylons, I trusted Gram's advice. I felt that I could talk to her about the silliest, most personal things without being ridiculed. And, after I talked to her, I felt that I, not she, had made the final decision.

Often I'd call Gram just because I wanted to talk. In mind's eye I can hear Donna chiding, "That's not surprising. You were such a motor-mouth you had to be talking all the time!" I'd tell her about my day at school or ask her questions about clothes or the way I wanted to wear my hair or what was coming up at church on Sunday—just chit-chat, girl stuff, things I couldn't discuss with Mom and didn't want to reveal to bossy old Donna.

Or I'd say, "Gee, I met this new friend at school. She seems to be really nice. Do you think I can bring her out for the weekend?" And Gram would say, "Sure, Janet. Of course you can," and out we'd go to be fluttered over and spoiled for a day or two.

Our first target at Gram's house was her freezer. She kept it full of popsicles that she ordered from the milkman who delivered to her house twice a week. I loved popsicles, even in cold weather, and never passed up an opportunity to devour them.

One summer my cousin Sandy Spooner and I were recruited to paint my Uncle Herb's walnut trees. The trunks of young walnut trees have to be painted with a mixture of diluted paint to prevent sunburn. We stayed at Gram's house and walked to Uncle Herb's orchard the following morning. I'll never forget how useful and adult Gram made us feel. Neither Sandy nor I were accustomed to a day-long work schedule and Gram didn't push us. I think we took a break every hour to get a popsicle, and every half-hour to get a drink of water.

Gram was full of encouragement. She told us what a good job we were doing each time we came to the house. Painting the trees became a game instead of a job. We'd go back to the orchard, paint a few trees, laugh, tell stories, and paint on each other. Then we'd scoot back to the house for another round of popsicles and return to paint a few more trees. We had the best time! And by golly, we got the orchard done and no one scolded us for not going any faster or for coming in the house so often to get something more to eat.

That kind of patience and understanding typified Gram's treatment of us kids. She knew we were going to get the job done—it was just a matter of how long it took us do it. It didn't matter to her that we spent nine or ten hours doing what Herb or Dick could have accomplished in two-and-a-half or three hours. After all, the trees got painted on the day they were supposed to get painted, didn't they? And, even more importantly, Sandy and I had a great time doing it.

It was that knack for recognizing when to give people room and when to step in and take charge that made Gram such a marvelous—and valuable—ally. She gave Mom plenty of leeway, let her run her household, even make mistakes, without jumping in and trying to take over. She was persuasive, but never intrusive, and she believed that every person had, and would exhibit, good qualities if you have them the opportunity to do so.

Her openness and receptiveness made conversation easy. I remember going to visit her and responding to her questions, "Well how's school? Tell me about your classes," with a diatribe about one of my teachers.

His personal habits drove me bananas—I hardly could stand to look at him. "To begin with," I explained to Gram," he has bad breath—terribly bad breath. And he smells. No, really Gram, he does. He needs to wear some deodorant. And, God, he's got terrible dandruff. Gram, I'm telling the truth. I mean, the dandruff is flaking off onto his shoulders."

Gram laughed along with me. But she didn't make fun of the teacher as I was trying to do. Instead, she ended the conversation by saying, "Gee, honey, don't forget, maybe he just has a few problems and we've really got to learn to look at the good things that he does. Every person has good qualities."

Sure, Gram, sure. . . . I remember thinking here comes Lesson in Life #118, Courtesy of Gram Carriere. "Yeah," I said, "yeah, of course . . . " and dismissed the conversation and her little moral lesson. But the next day in class, I looked at the teacher when he walked to the blackboard, and I saw something besides dandruff and B.O. and bad breath. I saw a very real, living, breathing person who was intelligent and capable despite a personal handicap. . . .

Handicap?

I gasped as though hit in the gut. Half the class turned around to look at me. Quickly I shook my head and buried my face in a book. But instead of the page in front of me, I was seeing my parents through a stranger's eyes. I didn't want others to judge them presumptuously, without taking time to understand that what they saw on the surface was not the real, the complete, person.

And I realized, thinking about Gram and her moral lessons, how much she had learned from my mother. For forty years, she had seen how people looked at, regarded—even talked about—her daughter. She had accentuated Mom's good qualities and tried to instill self-confidence by encouraging her in the things she did, complimenting her, participating in her activities, praising her. As a result, she learned to look beneath the surface when she met other people.

Learning after all is a two-way street. We learn from our children as well as teach them. Gram obviously learned a great deal from Mom, and from the experiences that were created by having to deal with, and love, her deaf daughter. As a result, she became a stronger, wiser person. Fortunately for all six of her Enos grandchildren, she was able to impart some of this knowledge, this sharing, to us.

Special. It's such a key word. From the time that Mom was tiny, Gram had made Mom feel special—special, not different. Her trips home from school, whether summer vacations or Christmas, were special times— both for her and for Gram. Her dates with my father had all been very special, and her wedding was a special event.

Her children, these little girls and later three boys, brought into the world by Gram's deaf daughter, were equally special as far as Gram was concerned. She dedicated herself to the concept that these grandchildren would prove that Mom could do anything that any speaking person could do. In some ways, this "specialness" was a burden for us; we constantly had to be aware that we couldn't do anything that would hurt Gram or cause her to think badly of us.

Donna, if a bit precocious and a "smarty-pants" around adults, was attractive and popular within her peer group. She never lacked for a date come prom time. Peggy, on the other hand, was a leader of people who were genuinely caring and understanding. She was not intimidated by peer pressure. It was very important to her to do things for others even if it meant sacrificing the acceptance of "popular" people.

Gram, of course, was aware that Peggy had this special gift. As young children we would react to the attention that Gram would give Peggy by saying, "Gram always loved you best!" Deep in our hearts we knew she loved us all, but Peggy spent a great deal of time with her because I feel they are very much alike. They care for people!

In a town the size of Willows, with its high school of less than 600 students and a history of inter-connected families which have known each other for generations, high school events like football games and junior and senior proms assume an undue amount of importance. Everyone talks about them—or seems to. And everyone seems to have a son or daughter, grand-son or niece or cousin, who is the halfback or princess or queen or cheerleader and they talk about them in stores and offices and on the telephone. Peggy did not attend all the proms, nor did she receive the recognition from her peers that she deserved. I'm sure she felt like any high school student would feel, very left out and too proud to admit it. But this didn't keep her from putting her best foot forward. I'll best remember those days of Peggy with a great big smile and an appearance of always being happy!

Gram would invite Peggy to spend the night of a dance or prom with her and she'd do something special for her and tell Peggy, "I know how important you think these dances are. But there's going to be other times. You're going to have your chance. And when you do, you'll make the most of it. I know you will." And Peggy would feel better about herself.

As the "middle child" among the girls, Peggy had competition from both sides. She learned to give in to Donna when it served her purposes or to shrug her away when she had other plans, thus giving herself room for her own life and her own friends. Occasionally Donna would go too far, and hurt Peggy's feelings. I remember, when petticoats were popular and girls in Willows were wearing four or five of them beneath their skirts, Donna decided to outdo everyone in school. She took all of Peggy's petticoats and wore them as well as her own, leaving Peggy without any. "Oh, it doesn't matter," I can remember Peggy saying. But I knew it did matter a great deal. What she really was saying, in effect, was, "This is a fight I can't win. I'll just have to shrug it off."

Had Peggy been taller, or more buxom, or thinner waisted, she might have been able to ward off these depredations. But she and Donna were almost exactly the same size. Consequently, as is the case in many families where girls predominate, clothes were traded, stolen and handed-down with confusing frequency. Occasionally Peggy benefitted from these transactions. Once, after Donna had been chosen "Portuguese

Festa Queen" for an annual celebration in Princeton, a little levee-side town east of Willows, she either couldn't make it to the event, or decided at the last minute that she didn't want to go. She corraled Peggy and told her to step in and do it for her. When Peggy started to object, Donna pulled her into her room to try the new dress on. She clapped and complimented Peggy on how attractive she looked, and insisted that she would be a hit as the Festa Queen. Peggy relented and appeared as Donna's stand-in. Whether or not she enjoyed the Festa, I don't know. But the situation typified the relationship that had grown up between Donna and Peggy—Donna taking charge, giving orders, making commitments and Peggy, willing to bend her own life around the demands of others, concurring rather than putting up a fight.

Peggy occupied a special place in Mom's eyes. Whereas Donna took charge and, willingly or unwillingly, dealt with the Enoses, answered the phone, planned birthdays, and made sure each of us did our homework, Peggy became Mom's helper. She was Mom's special voice. Lacking Donna's authority, and less pressured by dealings with the outside world, she took special pains to get things for Mom, translate for her, talk to people with and for her. And whereas Donna felt burdened, Peggy actually seemed to like her role as an intermediary between Mom and the hearing world.

With Gram, too, Peggy had a special relationship. But Gram, like the Enoses, ran things through Donna that she felt belonged, as it were, to the head of the family, since Donna was the one who made most of our decisions. Sex education was one of the duties that Gram felt obliged to transmit.

Though open and receptive to our needs and impulses, Gram was nevertheless thoroughly and without question a product of her generation. She never talked openly about sex. Neither did Mom. The only sex education I received at home was a promise from Mom that she would talk to us about sex when we were twenty-one; she didn't have anything to say to us, nor did any of us have any questions that we needed to ask her.

Gram, however, did undertake the task of instructing Donna about the "facts of life." "Oh, I remember that afternoon so well." Donna laughed when she told me about it. "I was visiting Gram at her house, and she decided that we should go for a walk. I probably was only ten or eleven at the time, but even so I could tell that Gram was working up to something. You know how she was, always very controlled, making light talk at first, trying to put you at ease, before she worked the conversation around to what was on her mind."

The two of them strolled over the levee and down the road that bordered it, Gram doing most of the talking as they proceeded at a leisurely pace. Obliquely, but without stuttering or hemming-andhawing, Gram led into the subject of reproduction in animals and plants. Then she went on to the obvious comparisons with human beings.

"I couldn't understand any of it!" Donna remembered. "But I went along with what she was saying. I listened and frowned and nodded my head so she would think I understood. Probably I was a little bit too young to have anyone explain such things to me. I didn't understand the lingo at all."

Politely, a little puzzled but not particularly troubled or upset, Donna thanked Gram for the information and dived into her reward for listening: cake, cookies, ice cream or popsicles—Gram always handed out goodies to children who listened and learned. Donna didn't find her newly acquired knowledge to be either interesting enough or shocking enough to mention to Peggy or me. As far as both she and Gram were concerned, the subject was closed.

Apparently Gram expected Donna to carry the ball and pass along the lesson in sex education to the younger children. Certainly Gram herself never took me on any such "nature walks," either when I was nine or ten or when I was older. And Donna never bothered to sit down with us to tell us what she had learned. Like most kids our age, and of our generation, we learned what we learned about sex gradually, from other kids, ourselves and books.

But by the time that Rick took catechism, the nuns had begun to recognize the need for instruction about sex and told each of their students, Rick included, to go home and to talk to their parents about the birds and the bees. He was eleven or twelve at the time. Donna had just come home on break from classes at Santa Rosa Junior College. Since Rick couldn't—or didn't want—to talk to Mom or Dad about anything that subtle, he went to Donna.

Donna's eyes lit up. She'd just completed a health science class at college and felt that she knew everything that the boys would need to learn. "Get Steve," she told Rick, and took the two of them off into a separate room. As she closed the door, she cautioned the rest of us, "Hey, I don't want any of you guys coming in this room, okay? I want to talk to Steve and Rick about this in private!"

"Oh God!" Donna later told me, Rick just sat there hiding his face. He thought it was totally yukky! 'Oh, no, don't say that,' he kept interrupting. He didn't know what he was getting into and he didn't want to hear any more about it.

"But Steve was totally into the conversation. He sat there and added to what I was saying. He was really interested."

So again it was Donna who stepped in to play "mother" in a school setting. I doubt that Mom ever knew about that conversation. Or knew that her "little boys" were getting the low-down from old "experienced" Donna, who'd learned all about such things in a college class. Mom couldn't have expressed herself as well as Donna and many of the terms needed to be fully described not just mentioned.

Once, during the course of a conversation about my Mom, Gram confided, "She was away so much of the time at school that I felt as though I had lost her. Emotionally, I had all the reactions, all the feelings, that a mother should have. The only difference was, I didn't have a child."

I realize now that consciously or unconsciously, she attempted to relive those experiences that she had missed through Donna and Peggy and me. We became the talking daughters that she hadn't been able to nurture and converse with when Mom was young. She didn't, however, cast off her role as Mom's guardian angel. She continued to do many of the things that she'd always done for Mom: arrange dentist appointments, make small purchases, talk to hairdressers, etc. Over the years, as we were growing up, she and Mom combined to provide the six of us with an extended functional family in which each took an active, but exclusive, part.

Gram did not intrude on Mom's space, but assumed various responsibilities associated with the raising of the family. Donna, the oldest, was only nine when Steve, the youngest was born. Mom did all of the cooking, managed the kitchen, changed diapers, cleaned house (although at times, she was somewhat casual about its appearance) and took care of her six children.

Gram was our liaison, our talking parent, our link with the speaking world. She helped us with school work, told us stories when we were little, taught us our prayers, advised us what to wear, who to associate with, how to get along in a rapidly changing world. As Donna grew older, Gram relinquished a number of these responsibilities and Donna became Gary's, Rick's and Steve's "little mother." But despite her precociousness and assertive personality, Donna was more of a first sergeant than a commanding officer. Gram never relinquished her quiet, unassuming, but effective pattern of caring for her deaf daughter and her deaf daughter's family.

Because we grew up with mother and grandmother fulfilling separate but distinct roles, we girls responded to each without confusion. Gram didn't compete with either Mom and Dad, and to my knowledge, they never challenged Gram. Gram's presence was so unobtrusive that she didn't come between Mom's relationship with Dad. And Dad, on his part, never resented Gram or anything that she did. He considered her one of the family.

Thus the family structure was enlarged by both sets of grandparents. The Enoses provided the employment and financial backing which enabled Dad to function as an independent member of society, while the

Carrieres—and specifically Gram—provided support in caring for the children and answering our emotional needs. That both sides of this structure were dependable and permanent enabled Mom and Dad to achieve the goals that they set for themselves, the foremost of which was to lead a "normal" life and rear a "normal" family even though they were deaf.

CHAPTER IX

"C'mon! Get out of bed! Hurry! It's First Friday! C'mon, everybody, it's First Friday!"

Donna, first sergeant and head taskmaster, rattled my bed, then hurried into the boys' room to awaken them. First Friday! Lights blinked on throughout the house. "Don't see why we hafta get up this early," Rick grumbled but Donna pushed him into the bathroom. Peggy and I competed for mirror space. First Friday communion was a mandatory event for devout Willows Catholics and we all piled out of bed an hour earlier than usual in order to attend.

With scrubbed faces and in Sunday clothes, our stomachs growling because we couldn't eat breakfast before communion, the six of us hurried to St. Monica's, Mom and Gram in tow. The service was warm and reassuring, and we maintained our best behavior, anticipating the rewards which would follow.

The boys sat near the back of the congregation. As soon as the priest pronounced his last "Amen," they were out of their pew and through the door, heads high and little legs pumping as fast as they could go for the parish hall to get Aunt Zeta's rolls. We girls, though a little more dignified, weren't far behind. Halfway to the hall, the cinnamony odor of fresh sweet rolls caught our nostrils. "C'mon, hurry!" I urged, breaking away from Peggy and Donna to take my place in line behind the boys. Aunt Zeta, as always, had risen before the birds to put the rolls in the oven and to put a kettle of hot chocolate on the stove. The rolls were warm and gooey and the chocolate emitted little wisps of steam. We ate like eager beavers, chattering and trying not to spill crumbs or chocolate on our church clothes.

First Friday: how we looked forward to it! The priest and nuns, lauded our devotion, even though they knew that we were motivated more by cinnamon rolls than by deep spiritual needs. Yet the religious feeling was present, and developed naturally. From our earliest childhood, we six children accepted the faith, believed in it, practiced it as best we could. If Gram and others dangled little rewards before our noses and we responded positively, so much the better as far as she was concerned. The Church, for us, was not a hostile fortress populated by severe and unsmiling saints. It was, throughout my childhood, a center of activity that like school, helped us to grow and to define who we were.

Our First Friday breakfasts continued, even after Aunt Zeta no longer could cater to the bunch of us. Gram took over the hostessing after communion service, treating us to breakfast in a restaurant or with rolls from the bakery, which opened just in time to permit us to gobble down our goodies, wipe our mouths and fingers and head for school. "They were bribes, weren't they?" I once asked Gram and she laughed, gently.

"Oh, I suppose you could say that they were. But there's no law that says you can't be rewarded when you do what you're supposed to do. Besides, Aunt Zeta always enjoyed it. And so did I."

To a great extent, our social life—and that of the Carrieres and the Enoses—centered around St. Monica's Church. Papa was a motivating force in the Knights of Columbus, and Avo headed fundraising and building committees and donated heavily to church projects. Both Dad and Mom, of course, had grown up in St. Monica's. I think Mom feels comfortable at church. She seemed to look forward to Sundays—but of course we all did, for Sundays and going-to-church highlighted our social life.

Oh! the preparations that had to be made to get us to church on time! The squealing and shouting and racing around began on Saturday night. Into the tub, one after the other, we girls would go. We shampooed our hair and scrubbed ourselves until our skin was bright red. Mom caught each of us as we toweled ourselves dry and began combing and curling our hair. Meanwhile, Dad herded the boys into the tub and supervised the soaping and scrubbing of toes and knuckles and ears. The minute he left the room to get an extra towel or article of clothing, a water fight broke out and he'd rush back in, clapping his hands and voicing wordless—but significant—reprimands.

After we were all tucked in and asleep, Mom and Dad would decide what each of us should wear to church the next morning. They'd place clothes in the hall for each of us. I can picture it now: six pairs of shoes, each with a pair of socks tucked inside them, arranged from Steve's tiny—but shined—size three to Donna's modish new teenaged pumps. Above them on the hall rack, were our dresses and slips and petticoats and hats, and the boys' white shirts, ties and suits. Oh! we were a proud and spotless family when we stepped out on the sidewalk in our Sunday finery!

Of all Sundays, Easter was the most special. Every year Gram outfitted Donna and Peggy and me with new dresses and Dad, who has always been particular about his appearance, made sure that the boys were neat and immaculate, in suits and ties or turtle-necked sweaters. On Easter, I remember, Gram made look-alike dresses for Mom and the three of us girls: pink flowers on pink backgrounds, with huge Easter hats to match! Despite the fact that everything had been laid out the night before, Donna couldn't get her hair to look just right, and I complained that my belt pinched, and Peggy spilled something on one of her socks, Ricky and

Steve were darting around, getting in everybody's way despite Dad's attempts to collar them. As a result, we were a few minutes late leaving the house and five minutes late getting to church.

The service already had started. We stood in the back of the sanctuary, looking from one to another and across the sea of hats and heads that seemed to fill every single row of pews. Someone beside us—possibly the usher, I only remember that it was an old family friend—gestured to Dad that the pew in the very front of the church was almost empty. In none of the others was there space enough for a family of eight. Dad nodded, smiled, squared his shoulders and signed to us to follow him.

I wanted to turn around and run, but I had no choice: I had to follow him. Peggy gasped and tried to disappear, but with that hat she was wearing, no disappearing was possible. I wanted to die. My cheeks began to flush—before I was halfway down the aisle, they'd turned a cherry red. I wanted to rip off that huge pink hat that I was wearing, but I knew that would attract even more attention than leaving it on. Like a flock of gracefully flapping, oversized flamingoes, we four Enos women made our way through the middle of the congregation and knelt outside our front-pew to make the sign of the cross. I'm sure the service was at least half over before the glow in my cheeks receded to a normally healthy red. "Oh! I remember exclaiming to a girl friend afterwards, "I was so mor-ti-fied I wanted to die! Just die!"

I feel certain that Dad and Mom and Gram took us to Aunt Zeta's after church. We always went there on Easter Sunday, for not only did she bake wonderful cinnamon rolls, she also staged the biggest Easter egg hunt in Willows. Hundreds of kids, most of us related, showed up and tumbled and rooted and raced across her lawns and through her shrubbery gathering brightly colored hard-boiled eggs in little straw Easter baskets. There were candies and pennies and kisses for winners and losers alike—not to mention spilled refreshements, scraped knees, an occasional bumped head and a tear or two over spilled baskets or cracked Easter eggs. But in the joy of the occasion, all was repaired, replaced or forgiven. We kids dearly loved her.

These Church events—First Friday, Easter, communion, All Saints' Day, Christmas—tied our family to the community in a meaningful way. Gram, I think, maneuvered a lot of our participation in the events on the church calendar. Tactfully, she provided incentives (a much nicer word than "bribes"!) such as new dresses, new shoes, choir auditions, etc., to keep us interested.

I think she realized that the Church could be an ally in the raising of children. Certainly it reinforced our ambitions and ideals, and provided a value structure that we learned to follow. As the children of deaf parents who were pushovers as far as discipline was concerned, we could have run wild if there hadn't been restraints placed on us. Both the Church and

Gram, in different ways, fulfilled that function. While still very young, we each learned—and believed—that while we could get by with a great deal and fool our parents, we couldn't get by with a great deal and fool God. We didn't often try.

Because Mom was basically a stay-at-home and Dad was basically family oriented, we entered into both Church and non-Church holidays as a family unit. Halloween was a great event, particularly when we were young. Each of us had a sweet tooth and we would, on occasion, fight rambunctiously for the rights to a last piece of candy or slice of pie.

Part of the appeal that Halloween exerted was the fun of dressing up in elaborate, and sometimes outlandish, costumes. Once we girls were older, Donna would keep after Mom to start sewing this or fixing that and she'd quickly catch the spirit of the event. She and Donna usually outfitted Peggy and me while Dad, sometimes with our help, costumed the boys. I remember that one Halloween Gary, Rick and Steve all decided they wanted to go trick-or-treating as Indians. Dad tied a towel around their necks (he often gave them their regular haircuts anyway) and with scissors and his electric trimmer he cut all their hair except for a two-inch wide "Mohawk" that stood straight up on the tops of their heads. He daubed their faces and shoulders and chests with paint and grease and, laughing and teasing and shaking their heads, they fashioned loin-cloths and armed themselves with bows and arrows and went racing out to trick-or-treat. If one could judge the effectiveness of the costumes by the amount of candy that the boys brought home, one would have to say that they were very, very effective indeed!

Invariably, Steve was the star during such expeditions. I remember people saying about him, over and over again, "Isn't that the cutest little fellow you've ever seen?" He was a chubby little rascal, bow-legged and irresistibly huggable. He had a round face and big brown eyes and grinned at anybody who'd look at or speak to him. As the baby of the family, with three older sisters and a mother looking after him all of the time, he grew up assuming that the world and everything in it had been made especially for him.

A big baby at birth, he weighed nine pounds and 15 ounces, he fulfilled Dad's wish for a third son. *Keep things equal! Three of each!* he laughed and told people in sign.

All three brothers grew up with constant attention—Mom, Gram, sisters, and a proud and athletically minded father. They didn't fall heir to the responsibilities that descended on us girls when we were little. Donna mothered Gary in particular—he seldom did anything without her help, her consent, or her advice.

Rick was the ornery one. "Your father deserves him," Avo once commented, then laughed when I told him that the same thing had been said about him when Dad was a kid. Gram remembered the last parent-teacher conference she attended before Donna advised her that she would take over that chore. "I remember the teacher saying, "Martha, he is just a naughty boy! He'd be out on the playground and he'd pinch this one or that one and then pretend that he didn't even do anything. And the kids would cry and it would be 'That old Rick Enos!' who'd done it every time. Rick loved to play! Sitting down to read a book or finish homework seemed only to be a vision in someone else's mind. Having a good time and being with his friends was the most important thing in life.

Steve, on the other hand, was an independent little guy. He had a healthy curiosity and a lot of manual dexterity. Like his brothers, he was competitive and started swinging a baseball bat and making football tackles almost before he could walk. But once Rick, two years older than him, started school, Steve virtually became an only child. He wandered through the neighborhood, swatting fence slats with a stick and climbing the shed in our backyard, where he'd preside from the roof as the captain of a pirate ship or the pilot of a war-bound fighter plane.

Occasionally he'd wander into the firehouse next door. The firemen took a liking to him. They'd give him cookies out of their lunch pails, buy him cokes and listen to stories about his playground exploits. He watched them while away idle hours playing pool, fascinated by the click of the balls against each other. He had to stand on a chair to see the table, and took his first poolshots balanced that way. Without the chair, he had to stand on tiptoe to see over the edge of the table. The firemen laughed when a ball crashed towards him and he ducked. They kidded him, "Hey, you better be careful or we'll shoot your nose off!"

The firemen nicknamed Steve "Sambo" because he was such a chunky little fellow. They officially made him the firehouse mascot. "No, heck no," one of the firemen told Donna, "we don't entertain him, he entertains us!" They wouldn't listen to any protests that he was spending too much time there and insisted that he was a friend and didn't get in the way.

Steve made friends wherever he went. I can still see him sauntering around the neighborhood, a roly-poly little guy who could smile from ear to ear. Old and young alike stopped to talk to him. They'd pat him on the head, give him money, and laugh with—not at—him. Of course, everybody knew where he lived and who his parents were.

While he was still a pre-schooler, he discovered that his smile and big brown eyes could work wonders at the frosty stand a block from the house. All of us had access to money, and began handling it when we were quite young, but Steve could get by without it. He'd mosey up to the frosty stand counter, pull himself up on tiptoe, blink his big brown eyes and order a cone or ice cream bar—or even french fries or a sundae. If he didn't have enough change in his pudgy little fist, the lady who managed the stand would smile and tell him, "Well, you're a little short, but this time I'll let you charge it."

Charge it! What wonderful words! Combined with those eyes, and that grin of his, they worked wonders. The counter people simply couldn't resist him and gave him everything he wanted. Most of the time, he tried to pay for what he ordered, but he wasn't old enough to be able to count it accurately.

Since Avo lived close to the church, he often picked Steve up after catechism and drove him home. Or part way home: Steve remembered that Avo often just would take him as far as Butte street and let him walk the rest of the way, since the street led right to our house and besides it was good to walk, of course! Avo was fond of his pudgy grandson and usually handed him a dollar when he let him out of the car. In 1968, a dollar would buy a pretty hefty frosty stand snack; Steve wasn't bashful about taking advantage of it. He got fatter and fatter.

Like Donna, Steve had trouble with catechism. But unlike Donna, his problems were mainly with vocal, not with written, language. He spoke what Donna later called "code." Many of his words and expressions were so indistinct that they only could be understood by members of the family. Unlike we four "middle children," Steve, as the youngest, never had to make himself understood. Instead of learning from us, he taught us to use his infantile language. Since it got him what he needed, he didn't have to improve upon it and continued to talk a garbled sort of baby talk until he started school. Both Donna and I remember that we thought it was "cute," coming as it did from such an adorable little guy, and instead of insisting that he talk better we encouraged the baby talk. I'm quite sure that Peggy and Gary and Rick did the same.

Once his brother and playmate Rick started school, Steve spent a lot of time during his last two pre-school years in the house with Mom, despite his frequent visits to the firehouse next door. He signed well and didn't need to use his voice to communicate with her, so his oral language skills didn't develop as they might have if one of us girls had been home. Fortunately, once he started school, his teachers were patient with him, and he caught onto proper pronunciation and how to use language effectively.

Steve was so cute, and so personable, that I'm sure he would have been popular no matter who his parents were. But as "the Enos boy—his parents are deaf, you know, and can only talk in sign . . ." the community treated him as one degree more special than anybody else. To varying extents, each of us drew that kind of consideration—whether we wanted it, or not. Often it became annoying and frustrating. Throughout my girlhood, I was never sure whether catechism honors, school awards— even grades and friendships—weren't based in part on my parents' "unusual" disability. The boys, in some ways, shared those doubts, but they quickly proved that they could stand on their own—and then some—on the athletic field.

To that extent, I think achieving an "identity," a place in the community, as it were, was easier for them than it was for the girls. Sports, particularly football, basketball and baseball, are cornerstones of Glenn County life. High school stars are bragged about, compared and applauded; Gary, Rick and Steve each got a fair measure of notoriety and praise.

They also got a tremendous amount of support from Dad. He never missed a game in which the boys participated unless it absolutely was impossible for him to get there. And the boys, on their part, virtually grew up in the stands at softball or basketball games in which Dad, or his brother Frank Enos, or Herb or Dick Carriere were playing.

After Herb finished college and returned to Glenn to take his place with Papa in the rice and walnut acreages, he joined an organized Willows city league basketball team. He recruited Dad to play with him, even though Dad was in his late thirties or early forties at the time. "We always had a good team," Herb remembered, "and won a lot of games. When we'd get ahead, I'd put your Dad in. 'The Hammer,' we called him. I'd tell the other boys not to shoot, just feed Henry."

"He was amazing. He'd pump in the points. He'd shoot, we'd get the rebound, pass the ball around and get it back to him and he'd shoot again."

"He enjoyed it so much. He could score a lot of points and it was important to him. It didn't make much difference to us who put the points on the board—we usually were way ahead anyway. It was a great boost to his ego—sometimes he'd be high-point man even though he'd only played half the game. He really loved it."

"A couple of times, when he was going really well, I'd leave him in for a long stretch. Remember, we played fast break basketball, and there was a lot of running involved. Even popping in all those points, Henry would get tired. He'd run past the bench and holler 'Unhh! Unhh!' and exaggerate how hard he was panting to show me that he was bushed and wanted to come out."

The Hammer. That was Dad. He'd make a gesture with his hand, and laugh. Everyone who played in, or watched, a city league game knew how to sign for The Hammer. He was one of the most popular players around.

Sometimes I've wondered how Dad would have reacted if Gary, his oldest son, had decided that he didn't like sports and had refused to try out for athletic teams. Donna, Peggy and I were in high school, and Gary and Rick in junior high, during the "Protest Years" of the 1960's when young people throughout America challenged the authority of the President and the morality of the war in Vietnam. Many of these clashes occurred in California, but not as much in the rural agricultural heartland where Willows is located. All three of Dad's sons were clean-cut

All-American types, and all of them shared his love for athletic competition.

Gary became a three sport star at Willows High. I remember, while I was still in school, that the varsity coaches began watching him when he was in junior high. By the time he was a freshman, he had cracked the starting line-up in football, basketball and baseball. And was Dad proud of him. Even Henry Enos, the State School for the Deaf's pride and joy, admitted that his son—his oldest son—had outstripped many of his own high school accomplishments. He'd corner anybody and everybody— on the street, on the farm, at family gatherings—and tell them about the tackles Gary had made in the Orland game, or the bases-loaded double he'd smashed off a Corning righthander.

Visiting schools sometimes would bring both their varsity and junior varsity teams to town to play. During football season, the JV game preceded the varsity game under the lights. But baseball games often were played simultaneously, the varsity on the main field behind the high school, the junior varsity on a field adjacent to it on the athletic compound.

This arrangement troubled Dad when Gary, as a junior, took over the varsity center field slot and Rick, a freshman caught for the JV's. Dad wanted to see both his sons play, and didn't want to miss any of the action, as he knew he would if he tried to run back and forth from one field to the other. After surveying the set-up, he hopped in his pick-up and parked it on a side street, at an angle, so he could see both fields. For two hours, while the two games progressed, he stood in the back of the pick-up, his binoculars to his eyes, and watched both Gary and Rick perform.

Boy, did my friends ever laugh about that! They thought it really was terrific that he'd go to that much trouble to see his sons play baseball. For days afterwards, I heard comments like, "Boy! I wish my folks took an interest like that in me!" and "Gees, my Dad never gets off work to come and watch me!"

This much appreciated support sometimes inconvenienced those who Dad worked with on the farm. The dairy business isn't seasonal and the Enos family, primarily Avo, Uncle John and Dad, although Dad's younger brother Frank was included in the business for a few years, did most of the work themselves. They also planted, maintained and harvested row crops; an absence at planting time or cutting time put a real burden on those who were left with the extra work.

All too often, it was Uncle John who got stuck with the extra effort. I won't say that he resented it, but I do know that he didn't like it. And Dad, I'm sure, was aware that he was creating a hardship. As John once told me, "A day or two before there is a ball game that he wants to go to, your Dad will start to fret. He knows that it's going to foul things up for the rest of us, but he won't give up on the idea. He gets into a guilt trip and becomes defensive, even angry. Finally he goes and when he comes back he tries to act as though nothing happened. Everything's fine as far as he's concerned—he hasn't lost anything."

Dad's insistence that he see every game in which the boys were involved was, I think, an outgrowth of choices he made when he was still in school and coming home during the summer. Already a good athlete, he'd begun playing with local teams and Avo had encouraged these contacts with the speaking world. "The guys," Uncle Frank recalled, "were just amazed at how he could react on the ball field. They didn't baby him and he competed on an equal footing with the best of them. That really helped him—and helped my Mom and Dad, too."

Also, Frank told me, "Avo would give Henry the keys to his car and Henry would take the Aguiar boys to Sacramento to watch the Solons, the professional Pacific Coast League Triple-A franchise. Avo knew what your Dad could do and trusted him to handle the car, be responsible, get back on time." That emphasis on sports, that living for the weekend when a baseball game would take place, or trip to Woodland to play for the Sacramento Silents, set values that Dad continued to live by for the rest of his life. With Uncle John, farming and the dairy business came first; sports were an occasional diversion to be indulged when one had time for them. Dad, on the other hand, worked in order to make a living, but sports—his hobby, his first love—provided the spice, the essence, that made life worth leading. Without them he might have become a dour and unsatisfied man.

Like so many boys who grew up in rural areas in the Thirties, Dad identified sports as football, basketball and baseball, one following the other through different seasons of the year. He also like to hunt and fish but these were separate outdoor activities and did not command the importance that the three major team sports did. Gary followed this pattern but Rick, two years behind Gary in school, got caught up in the "new" sport at Willows High School: wrestling.

Until the mid-Sixties, physical educations classes in North Valley high schools were largely recreational and consisted of spontaneous ball games, intermural contests and conversations with friends. Gradually an influx of college-and university-trained teachers introduced and taught more non-team athletic activities like gymnastics, swimming and wrestling. Dad never recognized them as "real" sports and seemed somewhat dismayed when Rick chose to wrestle instead of play basketball.

For the first time since the boys were big enough to throw a ball, Dad failed to attend one of his son's contests. He didn't go to see one of Rick's afternoon matches with a neighboring school, even though the event was held in the Willows gymnasium. He missed other matches later that same year, and returned less than enthused from those that he did see. But as Rick defeated opponent after opponent, and Dad caught the hang of the scoring and learned some of the fine points of competition, he became an ardent fan. *The best wrestler in school! Undefeated! Nobody beats him!* he'd sign to anybody who'd pay attention.

The boys' athletic accomplishments pleased Dad, in part because it brought him, as well as them, praise and recognition. He liked being told how good his sons were and, for that matter, how smart or attractive his daughters were. He always dressed well, walked with a firm, confident gait, smiled and put his best foot forward in public.

"Your Dad is so handsome!" I can remember friends running up to me. Or, "Your Dad has so much energy! He's such a neat guy to be around! Boy! I love being around your Dad!"

He came across to kids my age as a fun-loving guy who knew everything that they were doing. He knew the names of all the palyers on all the high school teams and he knew the parents of most of them. He'd stand outside the post office, his foot on the pick-up bumper, and with great animation talk about this touchdown or that free shot that somebody's son had made to win a game. He was a tease—but never a malicious one. He'd tell my girl friends how pretty they were or how nice they looked in church. I really felt privileged to have him for my father.

When my friends talked about my Mom they were likely to say, "Your Mom is so sweet!" She always was very good to my friends, and went out of her way to fix little snacks for them, or invite them to play in our house and yard—but she didn't go much beyond saying "Hi" and smiling. At most, she'd just talk, in sign, about the weather or something equally non-controversial and basic.

Nor did she pay a lot of attention to what other people in the community were doing. Sports linked my Dad to so many people, especially in Willows, which is so sports oriented. Mom, on the other hand, confined her social life to the family—her own and the enlarged family of which Gram and various Spooner and other cousins were members.

When I picture the big house where I grew up, I picture my Mom inside, sewing, cooking, perhaps just sitting and daydreaming, waiting for one of us kids to come home. She was a constant presence, warm and loving— she hardly left the house except to go with the rest of the family to church, or Gram's, or a ball game in which Dad or one of the boys was involved. On those few occasions when I came home and she wasn't there, the house seemed altered, as though not just a person, but part of its essential spirit, was missing.

One of those occasions really frightened me. I swung through the front door, books in hand, and stopped abruptly. The house seemed strangely quiet. The wind blowing a walnut branch against the side of the house seemed to whisper forbiddingly. I dropped my books and started towards the kitchen, then stopped abruptly. Oh! no! no! I remember gasping, then dropping to my knees to examine the spots on the livingroom carpet. Blood! Mom's blood!

I whirled and rushed out the front door screaming for Donna. She was half-a-block away, but came running. Together we rushed through the house, following the trail of bloodstains up the stairs, into Mom's and Dad's room, the bathroom, then the porch. Where was she? What had happened to her?

"Come on!" Donna shouted in my ear. "Let's go ask the fireman if they've seen her!"

No sooner had we rushed through the firehouse door, two very agitated wild-eyed teenagers, than one of the firemen jumped up and said, "I'll bet you're looking for your Mom. One of the veins in her leg broke and we took her to the doctor."

Donna and I virtually collapsed into each other's arms. The fireman explained that he didn't think Mom's injury was serious—as we hurried back to the house so Donna could phone the hospital, she remembered that Mom had been having trouble with varicose veins in her legs.

Apparently, while she was home alone, one of the veins had burst. I don't know how many minutes passed before Mom noticed that she was bleeding. She told us afterwards that it hadn't been painful, just "messy." She'd left a trail of blood throughout the house. Finally she'd wrapped her leg and decided that she needed medical attention.

I can picture her in the livingroom, a makeshift bandage tied around the wound, frowning. Dad was at work—she couldn't contact him, since she couldn't use a telephone. Nor could she call Gram. All of the kids were in school. She didn't drive so she couldn't take herself to the doctor or the hospital. Or go find Gram or Dad. She couldn't rush into the streets and explain the problem, for no one would understand her. She was completely isolated. Completely alone.

Yet she didn't panic. It was not as though she were locked in the Catholic Deaf School infirmary. She was home, among familiar surroundings. I picture her hesitating, thinking about Donna and the rest of us, perhaps even starting to write a note. Shrugging, she probably decided against it, limped to the closet to get her coat, went out the front door, down the steps and to the firehouse next door, where the firemen knew her and recognized her as their little buddy Steve's mother.

By the time Donna got in touch with Dad and Gram, Mom had been treated and one of the firemen had brought her back home. The condition wasn't serious, but, after thinking about it, I realized how vulnerable my mother was, even in an environment that offered so much companionship and protection.

CHAPTER X

The teacher blinked and frowned, momentarily puzzled, as though I were deaf and couldn't understand a simple spoken statement. "What do you mean?" I repeated, a little flustered that she should find me, of all people, interesting and unusual. Then she laughed and shook her head.

"So many deaf children grow up in a world surrounded only by hearing adults," she explained. "They never see deaf adults. They need to know that deaf adults do exist and that they can lead normal lives, work and raise families. Often the children of deaf adults are ashamed of their parents' disability. They never fully appreciate their parents or what they have done."

As I watched her and the children she was teaching I thought about my parents and how lonely and isolated they had been as youngsters. I smiled, realizing how much they had accomplished, and against such odds. No classes like this one in Oroville, only thirty minutes drive from Willows, had been available to them.

Here children three and four and five years old acquire pre-school skills that would lift them to equal footing with children who could hear. In addition, there were classes for adults who had children with hearing problems.

I'd gone to the school with my friend Linda, whose four-year-old son Joel was partially deaf. I had been teaching her and her husband Mike to use sign language and she wanted me to attend the school's parent-teacher luncheon with her. The hot March sun glistened against the brown fields that surrounded Oroville, an old mining town on the edge of the Sierra Nevada's foothills. Joel, confident and eager to join his friends, rushed into the school building as soon as we parked the car. Linda and I followed somewhat more demurely, and entered the school's auditorium-like central room. Kids were everywhere, signing to each other, their high-pitched voices reverberating with excitement.

After the pledge to the flag, in sign, the children were dismissed to go to their regular classrooms. One of the teachers, correctly assuming that this was my first visit, approached me and asked me about my interest in the school. My friend Linda explained that I wanted to meet her little boy Joel's teacher and see how he was doing. "She's teaching Mike and me how to sign," she added.

"You know how to sign?"

"Sure!" I laughed. "I've been signing since I was born!"

"Oh, my goodness! I want to talk to you as soon as I can get my class settled."

I told her about my parents, and she told me how many changes had been made in educating and training the deaf. With a gleam in her eyes, she exclaimed, "Janet, I know there were things that happened to you that other children never have and never will experience. People are yearning for the knowledge you have about coping with deafness in a family. You should tell the world about it! Allow others to understand the unknown challenges you faced as you entered this world."

Mom's and Dad's lives individually would have been easier, and less frustrating, if they could have taken advantage of the schools and the types of training now available to those with hearing problems. Modern technology has come to the aid of the deaf with captioned television, print-out telephones and accurate diagnosis of causes and treatment. Unfortunately, less progress has been made in the social realm. Both deaf children and deaf adults still tend to congregate together, in partial or total isolation, at odds with a speaking world that all too often considers them weird or funny or embarrassing or, worst of all, "dumb."

A better understanding of the languages of the deaf, both by the deaf and by those who work with them, has generated a marked improvement in communications between the two worlds. When I learned to read and write, a laborious process for anyone, I discovered, with both sadness and surprise, that I often couldn't read my parents' handwriting. It made no sense to me. Mom's, in particular, was all chicken scratches, the words and phrases mixed together, a verb where the subject should be and the subject between adjectives. When I was sick, or had a doctor's appointment, or needed permission to go on a field trip, I would write my own notes to the school attendance office and have Mom copy what I'd written and sign it. And I reacted defensively, embarrassed, when a friend picked up a note Mom had written and tried to decode it. I knew Mom wasn't dumb, but I couldn't understand why she couldn't write well—after all, I thought, writing has nothing to do with hearing.

Not until I was in my last year of college did I realize that the sign language that Mom and Dad had learned, AMESLAN (American Sign Language) was as different from English in its construction and word placement as a foreign language like Chinese. Like Chinese, it relies on associations of characters, rather than grammar. It condenses sentence structure, omits articles, prefixes and suffixes, and relies on facial expression and body language to convey degrees of involvement, superlatives and tenses. The sentence "I didn't get to work until noon yesterday because I had an accident. . . ." would, in AMESLAN, be formed with sign in this sequence: *Yesterday happened me accident work arrived noon.*

No wonder Mom's notes were so hard to read!

A newer form of sign, Sign Exact English, now is taught in most schools for the deaf. As its name implies, it formalizes sign into a system that parallels the structure and flow of English grammar (including "a" and "an," "the" and endings such as "-ing" and "-ly"). Sign Exact English does incorporate many AMESLAN features, however, and many deaf persons who use it throw in AMESLAN signs and short-cuts. But unlike my parents, they do not have to struggle with exact descriptions or ideas because they always can revert to exact phrasing and statements.

It becomes much easier, for example, for someone who knows Sign Exact English to paraphrase something they've read, or give instructions and/or ask or answer questions. As Uncle John pointed out to me, phrasing questions and passing on or repeating instructions were Dad's greatest communications problem on the ranch. His native language, AMESLAN, virtually was a code and a considerable amount of translation was required to restate or explain something in it. The language of the deaf is AMESLAN. Hearing people often feel Sign Exact English is better because it parallels their language and is easier to understand. A blend of each world, respecting each territory, needs to be examined.

Like many other children who have deaf parents, my sisters and brothers and I learned to sign before we learned to speak. "Home Sign", signs that only members of the families use for communication and generally would not be used by the deaf community, predominated our style of sign language when we were young children. Often times, "Home Sign" remained a part of our sign language even after we knew the correct sign. Sign language actually was our "native" language, and English a second, "learned" language. Of course, my college courses in sign were extremely easy for me, and I perceived how differently those who grow up with the deaf, speaking sign, and those who learn sign late, in order to work with the deaf, speak.

Deaf persons like Mom and Dad use more than signs to communicate. They use their bodies, their faces, their arms, their eyes. The most graceful among them literally transform sign into a personal ballet that often can be understood even by those who don't recognize or understand the significance of particular signs. They do not "speak" in monotones. They are exciting to be with, to laugh with and to talk to. Few speaking persons can tell a story, or describe a sequence of events, like they can.

Consequently, conversations in our family tend to be both loud and demonstrative. Dad and Mom get very vocal, particularly when they're excited, or caught up in the flow of the excitement; their noise cadences into ours. All of us kids can—and usually do—speak English and sign simultaneously. Put eight of us or, as sometimes happens, ten or twenty, or thirty counting aunts, grandparents and cousins in a room together and exclamation points really fly.

Dad, on one side of the room, will be "talking" pheasant hunting with the boys and Dick and Herb, his hands darting outward, invisible shotgun in his grasp. "Poom! Poom!" he vocalizes, his shoulder jerking with the recoil. The pheasant twists in flight—Dad's hands describe its downward fluttering—and falls out of sight. He goes after it but slips and sinks in the mud; the boys laugh; so does Herb. One of them interrupts but Dad out-noises him—there's more to the story: the bird isn't quite dead and bursts out of Dad's grasp, causing him to fall in the mud again!

Donna, Peggy and I interrupt; the boys laugh; Dad waves us away. The faster we talk, the faster our hands move. Herb perhaps, or Gus, Donna's husband, joins us on our side of the room. They and Clifford, my husband, start talking about the walnuts, or the house. Suddenly Mom, who hasn't said much, will interject, in sign *Did you read about the plane crash? It went right into the water! Boom! I don't know how many people were hurt.*

The conversation, for a moment, stops. We look at her. *Where did you learn about that?* I ask. *T.V.* she signs. *Where did it happen? Near here?* Mom doesn't know. Finally, Donna remembers that she saw something about a plane crash on the news. "It occurred in South America," she tells us.

Oh Mom! we laughed *why are you worried about that?* Dad, momentarily eavesdropping, can't resist *She reads about things and can't forget them.* Mom blushes and shrugs, laughs, looks at us. As she does, I realize that we've ignored her, or in our enthusiasm for the conversation we've stopped signing, and she's trying to join in. But, unlike Dad, who can concentrate on sports, she has no single topic that she can fall back on. Her attempts are genuine, and she's interested in what we're saying, but she often is a step behind us because of our lack of consideration to constantly let her know where we are in the conversation.

Harriet Wampler once commented that Mom sometimes was difficult to understand, even to someone who also knew and used sign. Harriet, of course, blamed the Catholic School in Oakland for Mom's deficiencies with sign—she didn't feel that Mom got a satisfactory basic education there. But Mom's personality, her passiveness, her uneasiness with strangers, also play a part. She lives in a microcosm of her own, a world in which she is surrounded by loving people who take care of many of the details of her life for her. As far as she was concerned, the plane crash was the most interesting event of the day. That it happened in South America made little difference to her.

My senior year in high school, Dad and Mom moved out of Willows to a farm just south of the little town of Artois. I was somewhat surprised to learn how much Mom liked it there. She told me *I can do what I want and nobody watches.* She has flowers, a lawn, a garden, and she loves to work outdoors with them. In town, she felt selfconscious about her deafness, and stayed in the house. As her big family suddenly dwindled in size, with daughters leaving to get married and set up housekeeping of their own and sons going off to college, she became increasingly restless. *But now I am happy* she claims. *All my children take care of me. I do the things that I want to do.*

Because she likes to work in the garden to raise flowers and vegetables, I bought her a gardening book as a gift. She liked it but she couldn't find anything in it about camellias, or azaleas, or whatever flowers or shrubs she was trying to raise. *Did you look in the index?* I asked.

She blinked then, in sign, asked *Index? What is that? Index* I repeated, then saw that she really didn't know what it was. I sat down beside her and turned to the back of the book. *See* I explained, pointing to the lists of topics. I showed her how they were alphabetized, and how the numbers across from them indicated the pages on which the material could be found. *See! there are your camellias!* I signed.

She gasped and clapped her hands. What a wonderful discovery! I laughed with her, realizing as I did so that many gaps like that exist for Mom—gaps that we, her children, never realized were there.

As a language, AMESLAN requires direct communications between speaker and "listener"; consequently, the deaf often lose the thread of involved or theoretical discussions. They don't absorb all the supplemental information that hearing people acquire. Language, for Mom, always has been informational, gossip, news— little one-of-a-kind tidbits thrown out, exclaimed over, forgotten. Invariably, when I'm talking to both her and Dad, Dad interrupts, finishes her sentences, corrects her descriptions, adds details to her accounts. Though good-natured, he is very impatient; conversation, to him, is an active, energetic, almost athletic undertaking in which the participants go full out.

Such outpourings of energy typify deaf gatherings. Like many deaf persons, Dad seems to key up when people are around. His head moves quickly, his eyes dart from one face to another. People meeting him for the first time find him to be over excitable, nervous, perhaps even insecure. But this, for the most part, is an illusion. Since he must use his eyes to "hear" with, he needs to see every expression, every sign given, every indication of anger, laughter, boredom, love.

Often he perceives things that hearing persons overlook. Often, when one of us kids would misplace a school book, or article of clothing, or a baseball or glove, Dad would know where it was. Either he had seen us put it down, or noticed it lying somewhere, and remembered what he saw. Details that hearing persons take for granted catch his interest and attention. I can remember him stepping forward to stop a noisy interchange among the bunch of us with a warning finger, break up an argument before it got out of hand. Though hearing nothing, he'd seen a scowl darken, a tear start, a hand begin to tremble.

This same "extra" sense, this accomodation to the lack of one sense with the heightening of another, makes Dad an excellent driver. He can "feel" an engine run, "feel" it kick over when he's trying to start it, see emergencies begin to develop before anybody shouts or honks a horn. I remember, as a kid, returning from one of our almost weekly summer trips to Stony Gorge Reservoir, a lake and campground in the foothills west of Willows. The sun was just going down behind the mountains as we weaved out of the hills towards the Valley. Suddenly I heard an ambulance siren. I whirled to look out the back window. The ambulance was shooting around the curve right behind us! We kids panicked, afraid it was going to crash into us, drive us off the road, or brake and skid because Dad couldn't hear it.

But Dad had "heard" it. He'd seen its flashing lights before we had heard the siren. Because of the curve, and the narrow shoulder, he couldn't move off the road, but he did slow down as he got around the curve. What relief we felt when the ambulance zoomed past us! Dad was unruffled. He knew what he was doing—he, not we hearing children, was in control of the situation. Mom, too, always demonstrated an extra perceptivity to feelings and wants. She knew when we felt sick, when we were disappointed or discouraged or afraid, before anyone else did. We couldn't conceal such things from her—fortunately, we didn't often try. And because she did perceive, and understand, she was the one we rushed to when we were hurt. She was the one who held us, comforted us, made us feel that we were loved.

I remember waking up about five minutes before the alarm was supposed to go off one morning when I was in the seventh grade. As I started to roll over, I screeched: I had terrifically bad pains in my right side. I hurt so much I couldn't believe it. I doubled over, whimpering. As Donna's and Peggy's alarms went off they got up, I called out to Donna, "Hey, I can't go to school. I'm just really cramped up and I don't know what's wrong."

Donna dropped what she was doing and came over to me. "Oh, boy, Janet," she smiled, "you're about ready to go into the world of adulthood. Your life is going to be changed now." She patted my shoulder and I nodded, teary-eyed and still whimpering. From her I'd learned about menstruation but I'd never imagined it would be so painful. I realized that I was going to do all those things she'd told me about, but I wasn't looking forward to it at all. Unfortunately, I didn't have any choice: Mother Nature was striking me. Rather vengefully, I thought.

Everyone left for school and I stayed in bed, doubled over with pain. Mom was real worried but she wasn't sure what to do. Finally I called Gram. I explained to her what was wrong, how badly my incipient period was hurting me.

Her voice softened. "Janet, do you need me?" she asked. "Would you like me to come in and see you?"

"I would love you to come in. Please, Gram."

She hopped in her car and drove in to our house in Willows. She checked me out and decided that I needed to see a doctor. She and Mom helped me to the car and Gram drove me to the doctor's office. Mom stayed home; Gram promised to notify her as soon as the doctor had examined me.

I remember hunching in the waiting room, trying not cry, until the doctor could see me. He told Gram he wanted her to take me to the hospital to run some tests. Gram helped me back to the car and drove me to the hospital.

Of course I was really frightened now. Gram sat in the little cubicle-like hospital room with me while we waited for the results, squeezing my hand very tightly and telling me, "Don't worry, honey. Everything's going to be okay."

The doctor was less reassuring. I was not suffering menstruation cramps, he told me, but appendicitis. He wanted to operate immediately.

I looked at Gram and burst into tears. She hugged me and whispered, "Don't worry, honey, don't worry." I remember that moment so vividly. We were right at the corner of the hall to my room to get me ready for surgery. I was bent over, in my robe. I poked at my eyes with my fist, sniffled, and took a big breath. "I think it's feeling better now," I told Gram. "I'd like to go home to my Mom."

She had to bite her lip to keep from crying with me. "Janet, you can't honey." She brushed my hair off my forehead with her hand and looked at me for a long time. "Honey, I'm so sorry I can't help you this time," she said finally. "You've got to stay here."

While the nurses prepped me for surgery, Gram left me to fill out and sign the necessary papers at the office. Apparently she made some phone calls and got someone to notify both Mom and Dad. Mom rushed in with tears in her eyes. I think she was as scared as I was. The nurses got me on the gurney and wheeled me down the hall towards the operating room. Just as we were passing the Emergency Room doors, my dad dashed through the doors in his work clothes. He'd just come off the farm and was really dirty. I could see his face looking down at me. It was the saddest, most expressive face I'd ever seen in my life. Tears filled his eyes. He bit his lip, touched me and signed *You're going to be okay!*

I burst into tears again. I was so glad to see him! The sight of him, and Mom and Gram, there in the corridor made me feel really special. As I closed my eyes, I knew everything would work out. With that kind of support, with that kind of love working and praying for me, it would have to be that way.

While I was in surgery, Gram took the entire family out for hamburgers. They had a big feast at one of the local restaurants. They all laughed about it later, and told each other, "Gee, we were having dinner while Janet was having surgery. That really was mean of us."

But of course it wasn't mean. It was a way of sharing needs and concerns. The entire family was together, all eight of them: Gram, Mom and Dad, Donna and Peggy and the three boys. Though I missed that feast in person, I felt that I was with them in spirit.

All of us were—and still are—connected by strong emotional bonds. Because they couldn't talk, and couldn't hear, my parents expressed themselves through their actions more overtly than the parents of many of my friends. Unfortunately, Mom and Dad sometimes misunderstood or weren't aware of more mundane concerns, like our needs as children and particularly as teenagers to be complimented and/or recognized for class-room or social achievements.

That I couldn't share thoughts, ideas—even praise from others, or compliments—conversationally with my Mom bothered me a great deal when I was in high school. I suppose, being the youngest of three sisters, all of whom were close in age, I subconsciously felt that I had to compete for attention. Donna had her role as first sergeant, and Peggy hers as Mom's helper. I sought approval outside the family. I was, by all accounts, a "goody-goody" in school. I liked helping the teachers; I turned in extra credit projects; I threw a lot of energy into everything from cheerleading to ski trips to student government to Catholic Youth Organ-ization fundraisers and luncheons. I enjoyed high school, and I felt successful doing the things that I was doing.

But I couldn't convey these achievements—or how much they meant to me—to Mom. Particularly, I remember being voted the "Good Citizen" award by my senior classmates. I was radiant and clutched the plaque, with my name on it as though it were the keys to Heaven. I rushed home so proud I could hardly hear or think. As I came in the front door, I saw Mom. I ran up to her and excitedly, in sign, I described how I'd gotten the award. She frowned, then tilted her head and smiled. For a moment I backed away, realizing that she hadn't grasped what the award—or my exuberence—was all about. I looked down at my hands as though the language they were speaking had betrayed me.

I tried, again, to tell her about the award and what it meant to me to win it but the language we shared—"our" language, sign— was in-adequate. All I could say was *The senior kids picked me for being good.* She smiled again, and congratulated me, but I felt cheated and deprived. Not by Mom, but by a language that didn't permit us to communicate on the same level that I could communicate with my schoolmates or teachers or Gram.

But for every "down" period like that, for every disappointment and frustration, there were "highs"—moments of great love and tenderness. Throughout my girlhood, until Donna graduated from high school and went away to college, she took charge of most family holidays. Or she and Gram worked in conjunction to plan and prepare, organize and carry through. A pattern developed so early in our family way of doing things that it was an outgrowth of the way that Gram always had looked after Mom and none of us ever questioned it. Gram and Donna bought our birthday gifts, arranged our Christmas shopping, planned the meals on Easter, the Fourth of July and Thanksgiving. None of us ever expected Mom or Dad to take the initiative.

My seventeenth birthday was no exception. I bounced home from school, delighted to be a year older and a year more mature, knowing that with Donna away in college my birthday gifts and birthday dinner would be Gram's and Peggy's inventions. Sure enough, they were there, bustling around, and Mom, helping in the kitchen, was unusually aflutter. The boys were quarreling over who would get the biggest slices of cake even before they'd seen it. Dad, home from work, was washed and natty in a clean white shirt and Sunday slacks.

"Happy Birthday" in song and sign preceded the blowing out of birthday candles. The usual birthday gifts were there—plus a special one, a big one, from Mom and Dad. "Oh!" I squealed, not really believing what I was seeing. *For me? You got it for me?*

They grinned and nodded—they'd picked it out themselves, they signed. I was floored. My eyes started to fog up as I tore the gift wrapping loose. I literally was speechless and my fingers hardly would function. Finally, I pulled a new piece of luggage out of the package. "Oh my God!" I cried to Peggy and the boys, "I don't believe it!"

I think that was the first present I'd ever received from them that they'd actually gone out to get themselves. I looked at them and my eyes filled with tears. I tried to shake them away but I was so happy, so complimented, that I couldn't restrain them. *Thank you! Thank you!* I signed. Then still wet-faced *I love you! I love you so much!*

I'd never felt so special in my life.

Such "highs" make me realize that I was, in many ways, a demanding adolescent. I needed a lot of approval and a lot of assurances. Gram, of course, helped and I often sought her out. I can remember going to her in a new dress, or a new combination of clothes that I wanted to wear, and asking, "Does it look all right, Gram. Does it really?"

"Oh, Janet, of course it does!"

"But really, Gram! Really! Do I look all right in it? Does it look good?

"Yes, honey. I just told you!"

"But Gram, I mean really! Oh, does it make me look good?"

And she'd laugh and shake her head, wondering how she could ever convince me.

If it wasn't Gram's approval I was seeking, it was a teacher's, or Donna's or a friend's. But sometimes, when I went to others, I was disappointed.

This language barrier created other barriers, too. In my quests for approval, I went to others and they sometimes made me feel less than special. All the way back to grammar school, I heard innuendoes like, "Oh, the teacher treats you special because your parents. . . ." Or, "You get all sorts of privileges because your Mom and Dad are deaf."

I didn't want assertions like that to be true. I worked hard for the recognition I achieved and I felt that I deserved the honors that I won. But even my best friends planted seeds of doubt. Just before an Award assembly, a classmate told me, "My Mom says that I deserve the awards but you'll get them because your parents are handicapped."

I recoiled, gaping. I was so surprised I couldn't think of a reply. Later, when I was alone, I started to cry. I was hurt and angry and stomped around telling myself "It isn't true! If I get the awards it'll be because I earned them! I've worked hard for them!

I did receive awards. And I know now that I deserved them. But at the time I wasn't quite sure. I'd always felt that teachers liked me and I liked them and I didn't feel they were giving me any special consideration because my parents were deaf. But throughout my life, people have confronted me with that possibility. Consequently, I've always felt that I've had to prove myself—do more than anyone else, or do things better— in order to get an equal amount of recognition.

Once in a while the boys got caught in this same syndrome. At the awards banquet, following football season the year that Gary was a senior in high school, he was named the "Most Valuable" player, the best offensive player, the "most inspirational" player and the team captain. Embarrassment showed in his grin each time he made a trip to the podium. He knew each award had been voted on by his teammates; nevertheless, he felt self conscious about receiving so many of them.

A few days later, the local newspaper—a weekly with small distribu- tion—printed an unsigned letter-to-the-editor criticizing Gary and the awards ceremony. The letter intimated that he should have refused some of the honors and suggested that the selections weren't made solely because of football achievements.

Gary was crushed. "I didn't ask for any of them!" he protested. "It's not as though I campaigned for them, or anything like that!" Those criticisms really stuck in his craw—and in mine. What do we have to do, I wondered, to prove we're as good as anyone else?

"Well, I know I spoiled Mildred. All of you, in fact," Gram told me several years later. "But I guess that worked better than just ignoring you would have done."

Yes, Gram, I can say now you did spoil us. Mom and Dad were special people, and they grew up under special circumstances. As Mom's and Dad's children, so did we. Throughout our lives we had to strive to achieve what others were granted at birth: the "normal" environment that hearing and speaking people accept as commonplace. On occasions, I'm sure, certain individuals did make concessions to us. Even so, such concessions were only slight compensation when compared to the disadvantages that beset Mom and Dad throughout their lives.

Being "different" can have a profound psychological effect on any individual. He or she reacts to the ways that he or she is treated differently and this reaction, or these reactions, shapes one's abilities to function. Mom and Dad have had difficulties with their environment, and each has been profoundly aware, throughout each of their lives, that they are "different" and, sometimes, "special." Because a support structure— parents, relatives, children, friends—built up around them, they were able to achieve many things, both material and social, that their contemporaries in the hearing world considered important. And through them and this support system, each of the six children has been given the opportunity to grow and achieve and, hopefully, to prosper.

As a family, we had our competitions, our hurt feelings, our tiffs and set-tos, but even as adults we have stayed together. Gary still goes to Donna for advice—after all, she was his "little mother"—and Dad already had begun to describe his grandsons as Major League baseball players and NFL football stars. All too frequently, I suppose, I swing through Artois to pick up my mother to take her to Chico to the dentist, or to Willows to do some shopping for her, or to go to Gram's for a visit. I go early, on special occasions, to clean her house or arrange a birthday party for Dad. Yes, as Gram spoiled her, we girls continue to spoil her! Often I run into Gary there or Rick or one of my sisters, and simultaneously in sign and English—and sometimes with a little Portuguese thrown in— we talk and laugh and share old times.

We are a family—a proud and, I hope, successful family. We love each other and have built a world worth living in. It hasn't been easy, particularly for Mom and Dad; I hope their confrontations and achievements, their struggles and successes, somehow and someday will prove valuable for others who must cope with hearing disabilities.

Our family reached its completion when Steve was born. I still vividly remember the first time that I got to see him. I was six, bright-eyed and mischievous, and Donna was already a mature and imperious nine. Mom, in bed, held Steve. Dad hoisted Rick to his shoulders from which heights he could pluck at curtains, light fixtures and fling imaginary spitwards at Gary, a rather serious five-year-old just a stairstep shorter than me. Peggy perched on the foot of the bed and Gram, behind us, stood in the doorway smiling. A ripple ran through the room—we each felt it, and reacted. Suddenly quiet, we interchanged glances, then simultaneously looked at Mom and baby Steve. *I love you* Dad signed, including all of us in the surprisingly gentle sweep of his hand. *I love you* we each signed back. Then, in happiness bordering on tears, we began to laugh.